Praise for The Art of Public Speaking

They say, Public Speaking is an art but oratory is the highest form of music. So one can say that great speeches have to be equated to great acts of performing act. This book is a wonderful guide for a road to achieving excellence in this all important endeavour of our life.

I myself have done a considerable amount of Public Speaking – the audience ranging from ten to ten thousand, the venues varying from Harvard to Hanoi, from Beijing to Brussels and from Chiplun to Chennai. But I must say, I myself learnt some new tips after reading this insightful little book.

R. A. Mashelkar, FRS
President, Global Research Alliance, Chairman, National Innovation Foundation, National Research Professor.
***

The book touched a difficult task in to "Art" of doing the things. Those who take pains to read, would not only immensely benefit; but would enjoy it too.

Dr. Arun Nigavekar
Raja Ramanna Fellow,
Former Chairman – UGC, Former VC – Pune University.
***

The book is designed as a guide to the art of speaking. Interspersed with examples, anecdotes as well as do's and don'ts, make the book interesting and easy to grasp. Since each of us might not have the 'gift of oratory' or be a born speaker, the book presents tips and tricks for developing this important art. With extracts of speeches by great orators, the authors provide guidance to the readers for preparing their own speeches. The authors also explain very lucidly that speaking is not just about words, but also several non-verbal techniques.

I applaud the authors for conceptualising this book and writing it in a practical manner to suit both, formal and informal settings.

Air Marshal Bhushan Gokhale PVSM AVSM VM (Retd)
Former Vice Chief of Air Staff
Indian Air Force

***

Indian wisdom of civilization puts the ratio of orators to people as one in thousand – "Vakta Dash Sahastreshu" The book seeks to improve this ratio by making oratory an accessible, learnable skill for everyone who wish to develop Public Speaking. You can use this book as a self learning manual. This book draws on wisdom from ancient Greek, Roman and Indian civilization to modern Corporate World. This oratory is rooted here in Bharatiya Sanskriti and I would like to say therefore, it has a universal appeal. A study and reading of this book will make you; a better Public Speaker.

Avinash Dharmadhikari (Ex-IAS)
Director – Chanakya Mandal Pariwar – An Open Education System

***

The Art of
Public
Speaking

Mukund Puranik

Shilpa Nazar

Diamond Publications

The Art of Public Speaking

Mukund Puranik, Shilpa Nazar

First Edition : February, 2017

ISBN 978-93-86401-04-5

© Mukund Puranik, Shilpa Nazar

Cover Page
Sham Bhalekar

Typesetting
Diamond Publications

Published by
Diamond Publications
264/3 Shaniwar Peth, 302 Anugrah Apartment
Near Omkareshwar Temple, Pune - 411 030
☎ 020-24452387, 24466642
info@diamondbookspune.com

For Online Shopping Visit to
www.diamondbookspune.com

Sole Distributor
Diamond Book Depot
661 Narayan Peth
Appa Balwant Chowk
Pune 411 030
Tel. - 24480677

Dedicated to

Late Mr. GANESH DATTATRAY PURANIK

Ever Adorable Father of Shilpa
&
Beloved Brother of Mukund

Preface

"I shall prefer "a book" to heaven because heaven emerges with the reading of a good book. With the help of a book, a heaven is created even in hell!" – Lokmanya Tilak.

The world of books is the most remarkable creation of a man, nothing else that he builds ever last, monuments fall, nations perish, civilizations grow old and die out, and after the era of darkness, new races built others but in the world of books are volumes that have seen this happen again and again and yet live on, still young, still as fresh as the day they were written still telling men's hearts of the hearts of men centuries dead. Reading and learning has liberated more people than all the wars in the history!

Every budding writer, writes and runs around showing what he wrote. We are no different than this usual vision. We too found something and we have the same eureka feeling of Archimedes. Hope our honourable readers will accept what we have penned down.

At a minimum, the first twenty years of our lives are spent as learners and receivers, as members of the audience. But there comes a time when, we turn around and become givers, teachers and leaders. Today's youngsters are the future builders of society. It is imperative that they should read biographies of great people and chisel their thinking on the path of lofty ideals. The great personalities have left messages of lasting value. A sincere glance of the same should rekindle the interest of youth in understanding the noble thinking of the great personalities.

But our optimism does not stop here and hence we pray that: Let this book be the satisfaction and delight of old and the regular diet for youth. Let reading of this book prove to be a step in; and open the door to the world of creative thoughts and imagination.

Acknowledgements

I will be honest here: I have been forced to write this book! Not that I did not relish writing it but my actual research and writing went on for more than a year and it was only after gentle reminders from my dearest uncle and the co-author of this book, Mukund Puranik, that I sat down 15 days back, stopped further writing and started the assembling work.

My language skills – I owe them entirely to my father – my Baba! His constant endeavour had been to make voracious readers out of both his daughters and he succeeded like no one! Thus began my love affair with books (and the only one that Baba ever approved!!) and it has lasted this long. My mom, Mrs. Sudha Ganesh Puranik, has been a pillar of strength to her daughters. And my sister, Dr. Krittika Moghe, has been both the proverbial elder sister and a best friend!

I express my gratitude to my husband, Mangesh and my son, Aditya. Mangesh, thank you for not complaining even once about sleeping with the lights on! Thank you Aditya, for letting me sit through entire days at a stretch, though I was not very happy with our deal of trading your 'Mom'-time with McDonald's!

Shilpa Nazar

I extend my sincere thanks to Wife Jyoti, Daughter Neha & Son Vivek for not only complimenting my love for English Language but whose encouragement gave me the eyes to see its grace.

Mukund Puranik

Here comes the important question: Is this book great? Or does it grate? We want it to be great!

Table of Contents

1. Introduction

Jerry Seinfeld has famously quoted, "A study that said speaking in front of a crowd is considered the number one fear of the average person. We found that amazing! Number two was death! Death is number two?? This means to the average person that if you had to be in a funeral, you would rather be in the casket than doing the eulogy!"

A very popular quote, used too often and misquoted as is. The basis for the quote came from the 1977 edition of The Book of Lists which stated that 41% people feared speaking to a group while only 19% feared death. This appears to have its origins in a 1973 study called The Bruskin Report which stated that in a survey sample of more than 2500 Americans, 41% feared public speaking.

The study and survey findings are more than 40 years old and as such do not stand ground in today's world. But this does not negate the fact that people are indeed more fearful of speaking to a group / audience. While comparing the fear of public speaking with fear of death or fear of heights or fear of spiders is not valid, fear of public speaking remains one of the top fears. There are more people who have this fear more than any other. Many of the 'normal' people struggle with it every day.

So what exactly constitutes public speaking? And how is it linked to oratory?

Public Speaking is the process of communicating information by directly speaking to a live audience. An audience is a group of listeners, like in a school or a workplace or in our own personal lives and the intention of the speaker is to inform, influence and / or entertain the audience.

An orator is a public speaker. Oratory is persuasive public

speaking. It seeks to convince the listener with its theme. It is delivered with passion and conviction, appealing to the sentiments and emotions of the listener, tugging at the heart strings of the audience and often inspiring righteous action.

The power of the spoken word is undeniable. There have been great orators since time yonder, like Demosthenes, Cicero, Julius Caesar in the Greek and Roman world. Great speeches have motivated ordinary citizens of a country to fight against injustice and lay down their life for a worthy cause. Politics have been influenced by great orators and great speeches like Winston Churchill and his 'We Shall Fight On The Beaches', Kennedy and 'Ask Not What Your Country Can Do For You', Martin Luther King and 'I Have A Dream'. Closer home, Jawaharlal Nehru's 'Tryst With Destiny'still brings tears to the eyes. Atal Behari Vajpayee, a man of impeccable rectitude and integrity has been a tall personality in politics and oratory field. The effectiveness of his talks has been determined fundamentally by his sheer love for his country and his poetic mindset. His speeches have always been a treat. His thoughts touch the listener's heart and are like magnetic signals that draw the parallel back to you. Present Indian Prime Minister, Shree Narendra Modi has showcased his greatest talent in his oratory skills. One may or may not believe in his ideology but it is an acknowledged fact that he is an outstanding communicator who has the pulse of the nation. His speeches have been crowd pullers and fodder for conversations and debates. His ability to connect with his audiences has often inspired positive action from the masses. Indian Prime Minister's style of audience engagement is perhaps only second in the world to none other than the President of the United States of America, Mr. Barak Obama. Barak Obama has a more global appeal and is unequivocally one of the greatest communicators in the world. Critics argue that it is more style than content in his speeches. But no one can deny that it is his way of connecting with his audiences, be it a group of school children, the masses or his senate, rather than his policies, that has put him in the White House two times.

However, the power of spoken word can be used for malevolent purposes and to convince the audience to indulge in nefarious activities, against the very nature of a social fabric. Hence there remains a greater responsibility with oratory and orators. An orator can become a voice for social and/or political change.

Simply put, all public speaking does not make oratory but the otherwise is true. For example, a teacher in her class, a political speech or a speech at a graduation ceremony is not oratory but it can be raised to that level.

In today's fast paced world of social media networks, communication has dwindled down to getting a message across in a few mere characters. Emoticons are used copiously to express instant (read: instant and forgotten within the next few seconds) emotions. Does this mean that our voices will become extinct? The power of face-to-face communication cannot be denied. There is still hope....

2. History & The Art of Speaking

Human beings have long left behind them the cave days when action rather than speech occupied a larger part of their lives, and are now closely interrelated units in a civilization which is held together by constant communication between the millions across the globe. No one is alone; each is dependent on others. Everyone must reach out to everyone. How do we do this? We do this by spoken words.

History

The Hellenistic period is the period in history defined as the time between the death of Alexander the Great in 323 BC and the rising power of Roman Empire in 31 BC. This period was known for its advancements in philosophy, literature, arts and science. During this time, the Greek culture was dominant throughout the Mediterranean. Oratory and rhetoric were key components of the Greek culture. The Hellenistic World was an oral communication culture, with public performances and lectures as its primary literature in those times.

Oratory was considered as one of the highest arts and a virtue. The orator was a celebrated figure in the society, and rhetoric, the art of the spoken word, was a strongly valued element of the classical education, with the most highly educated receiving particularly strong rhetorical training.

Demosthenes of Athens was the first known tall figure of oratory. He was a Greek statesman and an orator of ancient Athens. And he developed this art by his untiring efforts. He had to remodel his thin voice. He underwent a disciplined program to overcome his weaknesses and improve on his delivery, including his diction, voice and gestures. He read and wrote history volumes of Thucydides, umpteen times. Ultimately he became the history himself in the art of oration. This lone example testifies that oratory power is not always gifted but obtained through diligent preparation. It is understood that the oratory power over a period of time got structured into a science in a sense that the subject matter of the speech received a set form and a structure.

Oratory began to flourish in Rome when the Roman Empire conquered Greece and started following its traditions and culture. The leading Roman families often sent their sons to study under a Greek master, as happened with Julius Caesar. The Romans were less intellectual than the Greeks but their speeches had more style and stories. Cicero was one of Rome's greatest orators. Oratory was on a decline during the Renaissance and the Middle Ages, where it was largely confined to religious discourses.

In ancient India, debates on national and social issues were a common phenomenon, wherein the Pundits (the experts) used to gather for what was known as a Pundit Sabha. It was a debate, where one-upmanship on a particular subject was considered as an achievement for Pundits. Shankaracharya, Mandan Mishra, Gargeyi, Kumaril Bhatt, Nagarjun were some of the known names in the field who had captivated the audiences and literally captured the Sabha's by their oratory skills. The wisdom of Shankaracharya, the arguments of Mandan Mishra and Gargeyi was a feast of words for the listeners. Sanskrit was the language and Dharma (the eternal law of the Cosmos) related subjects were the agenda of the debates. But there was no mass participation in such debates. And the absence of enthusiasm from general masses impeded the development of this art in ancient India. The art never got picked up by the masses and more or less remained confined to the elite circles. Ancient India also boasted about the prowess of the great strategist Chanakya and the great emperor, Ashoka who propagated Buddhism throughout Asia. History is a witness to the fact that it never influenced and helped the Hindu Society in general for its good moulding. In the more recent times, Pandurang Shastri Athavale was a spiritual leader, philosopher, social activist and reformist.

He was famous for his discourses on the Bhagvad Gita, the Vedas and the Upanishads.

The preachers are invariably good orators. There exists in any society Saints and Philosophers who preach. It is said that saints practice what they preach. What the saints preach comes out of their self-attainment and rich experience. Hence the saints enjoy a larger sustained following. They preach not for the sake of preaching but as a mission and for the ultimate good of masses.

There have been notable orators at the turn of the century, who delivered rhetoric with conviction, knowledge and confidence and it made them famous. While Winston Churchill, John F. Kennedy and Martin Luther King Junior were powerful and inspirational speakers, Adolf Hitler's incredible ability to sway his audience to working in his favour speaks volumes about his communication skills.

The art of oratory has seen a steady decline since and while we do have few good speakers, it is about time to resurrect this art again and become the confident communicators we wish to be.

3. Communication

There is no such entity in existence, such as a born public speaker. Public Speaking is an art. It needs to be learnt, practised and developed. We often watch celebrities, politicians, or business leaders speak on television or in public, and wonder how do they seem so much at ease?! Are they great speakers or are they just born that way? A very few individuals are born with this gift, while the overwhelming majority of popular public speakers train themselves to be so effective. If one wishes to be an outstanding communicator / speaker, they have to acquire the know-how of public speaking skills. One can take heart from the experience of others and achieve their dreams. The ability to communicate effectively comes with proper training and correct practice.

There are five essential attributes a person must cultivate to be a good speaker. First and foremost is the initial urge, the yearning from within to become a great communicator. Unless you yourself want the change to happen, it won't happen. Second step is reading and acquiring knowledge from varied sources, everyday happenings, books, newspapers and internet. The world is shrinking at a faster pace with respect to the information available. Converting this information to useful knowledge will help you in applying it in various speaking and communication situations. Third is developing the literary excellence which is practising writing and practising good writing. Remember – practice makes perfect when we practise the correct things! Number four is courage. Winston Churchill has famously said "Courage is what it takes to stand up and talk. Courage is also what it takes to sit down and listen!" Number five is to get trained from professionals. Professionals train the trainee speaker by giving emphasis primarily on style and voice culture. For instance, experts tell us that anyone wanting a heavy voice can try to get it by shouting from the top of their voice on a sea shore facing the sea. In one example, a girl from the neighbourhood who was in habit of reciting poems in a louder tone before the mirror, later went on to become a good speaker on the platforms of leading student union. Many have witnessed her travelogue in that oratory field. She possessed that desire to be successful and achieved it with perseverance, hard work and proper practice.

Normally, in ordinary conversations, people are articulate and at ease and in their comfort zones but when faced with the prospect of addressing a group, their self-confidence invariably get smashed into pieces. But there is no public speaker, no effective communicator in professional life who has escaped the early tremors. There are tools that deal with public speaking and fear as the basic problem. The tools are a synthesis of techniques derived from three different fields – Behaviour modification, Acting mode and Speech crafting – in order to gradually change a fear response to a controlled response. The biggest skill one can acquire by using these techniques is Fluid Response – meaning a person will be able to respond clearly and comfortably to questions, interruptions, distractions and unplanned happenings during the course of a speech / presentation.

Communication

Communication happens when two or more people exchange information and ideas, share their views and perceptions, and swap opinions and thoughts. We humans are an unpredictable lot! We are not passive beings who will always interpret a communication in the "correct" way and give a expected reaction. We would become boring then!! Communication is an active process which is hugely influenced by human's complex behaviour and different thinking patterns.

Communication skills are important to each and every person, in order to be more effective and convincing; in the way we put forth our message, ideas and opinions to others.

Technically speaking, communication is transmitting and receiving information from a sender to a receiver, through a communication channel. It is categorized into two types:

- Verbal Communication
- Non-verbal Communication

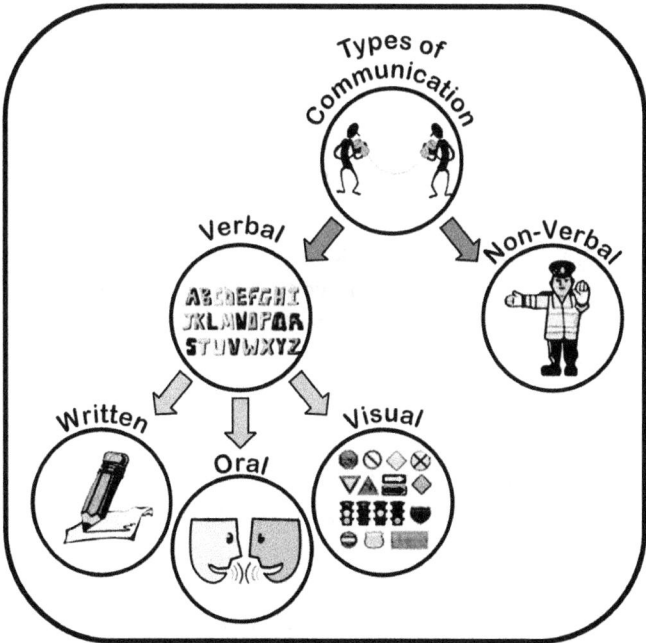

Verbal communication

This is accomplished by using writing and speaking skills to convey our messages. This is the most successful form of communication, making the process of communication easier and faster for us. It is further categorized into:

- Written
- Oral
- Visual forms of communication

Written communication is through pen-and-paper, emails, faxes, text chats, SMS. The effectiveness of this type of communication very much depends on the style of writing, grammar, vocabulary, clarity and precision of instruction. The pluses here are that the message text can be edited and revised before it is actually sent, it can be saved for later use, and it is easy to obtain feedback from the receiver in as unambiguous way as is possible. The downside is that one may not always receive instant feedback, as people may struggle with vocabulary and writing ability.

Oral communication involves face-to-face communication, telephonic conversations, speeches, presentations, radio and voice over internet. It can be informal like having general conversations or formal like speech, presentations and conferences. Its effectiveness depends on voice energy, voice clarity, voice modulation, volumepitch, speed of spoken words and also on body language and visual cues. When we talk to others, we often assume that others understand what we are saying because we know what we are saying. But usually this is not the case. People bring their own attitude, perception, emotions and thoughts about the topic and this creates barrier in delivering the right meaning. The plus is we can receive instant feedback. Unlike written communication, there is never enough time to think and react. So it is very likely to end up in regrets. As it is said in a famous proverb – "We are masters of the words unsaid and slaves of those we let slip out!"

A picture is worth a thousand words! **Visual communication** encompasses pictorial elements used for communicating our content. Human beings are very graphical

3. Communication

There is no such entity in existence, such as a born public speaker. Public Speaking is an art. It needs to be learnt, practised and developed. We often watch celebrities, politicians, or business leaders speak on television or in public, and wonder how do they seem so much at ease?! Are they great speakers or are they just born that way? A very few individuals are born with this gift, while the overwhelming majority of popular public speakers train themselves to be so effective. If one wishes to be an outstanding communicator / speaker, they have to acquire the know-how of public speaking skills. One can take heart from the experience of others and achieve their dreams. The ability to communicate effectively comes with proper training and correct practice.

There are five essential attributes a person must cultivate to be a good speaker. First and foremost is the initial urge, the yearning from within to become a great communicator. Unless you yourself want the change to happen, it won't happen. Second step is reading and acquiring knowledge from varied sources, everyday happenings, books, newspapers and internet. The world is shrinking at a faster pace with respect to the information available. Converting this information to useful knowledge will help you in applying it in various speaking and communication situations. Third is developing the literary excellence which is practising writing and practising good writing. Remember – practice makes perfect when we practise the correct things! Number four is courage. Winston Churchill has famously said "Courage is what it takes to stand up and talk. Courage is also what it takes to sit down and listen!" Number five is to get trained from professionals. Professionals train the trainee speaker by giving emphasis primarily on style and voice culture. For instance, experts tell us that anyone wanting a heavy voice can try to get it by shouting from the top of their voice on a sea shore facing the sea. In one example, a girl from the neighbourhood who was in habit of reciting poems in a louder tone before the mirror, later went on to become a good speaker on the platforms of leading student union. Many have witnessed her travelogue in that oratory field. She possessed that desire to be successful and achieved it with perseverance, hard work and proper practice.

Normally, in ordinary conversations, people are articulate and at ease and in their comfort zones but when faced with the prospect of addressing a group, their self-confidence invariably get smashed into pieces. But there is no public speaker, no effective communicator in professional life who has escaped the early tremors. There are tools that deal with public speaking and fear as the basic problem. The tools are a synthesis of techniques derived from three different fields – Behaviour modification, Acting mode and Speech crafting – in order to gradually change a fear response to a controlled response. The biggest skill one can acquire by using these techniques is Fluid Response – meaning a person will be able to respond clearly and comfortably to questions, interruptions, distractions and unplanned happenings during the course of a speech / presentation.

Communication

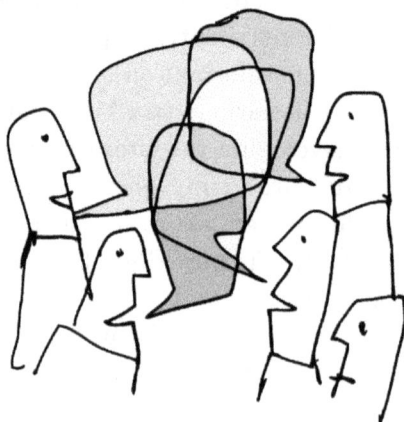

people. We remember what we see more easily than what we read or what we hear! Graphs, charts, infographics, images and maps are some of props that make the written word easier to understand.

Non-verbal Communication

Interpersonal communication is much more wider than the actual spoken word and its explicit meaning. It includes implicit meaning which is conveyed through nonverbal behaviours. This is communication without words. It includes outward behaviours such as facial expressions, eye contact, gestures and tone of voice, as well as less obvious messages such as dress, posture and spatial distance between two or more people.When a person is speaking, we can notice the changes in facial expressions and respond accordingly. Examples of this type include shaking hands, patting the back, hugging or other kinds of touch. It takes in formal and informal communication.Facial expressions can convey the speaker's emotions correctly when used in sync with the words. They help to reinforce an important message or an idea. Eye contact helps the speaker to make the situation an all-inclusive event where the audience feels that it is valued. Gestures and tone of voice help the speaker to highlight important words or sentences and can be used as signals to the audience.

It is essential to develop both communicating and listening skills in order to be understood as well as understand correctly. Knowing the audience and understanding how do they want the message to be delivered is as important as knowing yourself and your subject. Rather the former outweighs the latter!

This is even more important in the corporate world. *"Communications Skills"* is a phrase repeatedly used in job descriptions and resumes. One of the most important communication skills is the ability to present our ideas clearly. These skills – or the lack of them – can make or break an individual's career.

Why is Public Speaking an important skill to learn?

Not everybody needs to make regular presentations in front of an audience. However there are plenty of situations where good public speaking skills can help one to advance one's career and create opportunities.

For example, you might have to talk about your organization at a conference, make a speech after accepting an award, or teach a class to new recruits in induction. It may include online presentations or talks, like training a virtual team, or speaking to a group of customers in an online meeting.

Good public speaking skills are important in other aspects of our life too. You may be asked to make a speech at a friend's wedding, give a eulogy for a loved one, or inspire a group of volunteers at a charity event.

While it is true that good communication skills can open doors to different opportunities, the opposite can happen with poor skills. For example, your boss might decide against promoting you after sitting through a badly-delivered presentation. You might lose a valuable new contract by failing to bond with a prospect during a sales pitch. Or you could make a poor impression with your new team, because you stumble through your words and don't look at people in the eye.

A good understanding of the different types of communication and communication styles can help every person know and deal with people better, clear up misunderstandings and misconceptions and contribute to the success of their enterprise. The ability to communicate effectively with every other person can win cooperation at work. Anyone who wants to move up the ladder in their career should incorporate these invaluable attributes to their personality. Think about the satisfaction that you will get when you stand up and confidently share your thoughts and feelings with the audience. And no matter how experienced a speaker is, he / she should always have a healthy dose of anxiety that his / her matter is well made for the occasion.

In summary, being a good public speaker can enhance your reputation, increase your self-confidence and open up numerous opportunities.

Let us all learn how to speak well!

4. Body Language, Voice & Content

Imagine an audience in a typical business presentation situation. A few are physically present but mentally somewhere else. They could be thinking about their sick child at home, or the 200 emails that need to be answered or the argument they had with their partner at home that very morning! Some may have flown directly into the city from an earlier assignment and are still jet-lagged. While we would like our audience members to pay complete attention and soak up each and every of our word, they are simply not prepared to do so! They come with their own baggage of emotions, thoughts and conflicts. We have a job to do here – we have to earn their attention and then retain it all the way till the end!

A vast majority of us communicate messages without using speech quite often. A theory on the origin of language has tried to establish a fact that speech originated from gestures. For example, we nod our heads to show approval or shake our heads to indicate disapproval; in a conference or training situation, we often put our hand up / show our hand to indicate that we want to ask something or offer a comment on the topic being discussed. In fact, communication experts point out that only a small percentage of communication is verbal whereas a large percentage is through body language.

Verbal:
The Story You Tell

7%

Vocal:
Voice

38%

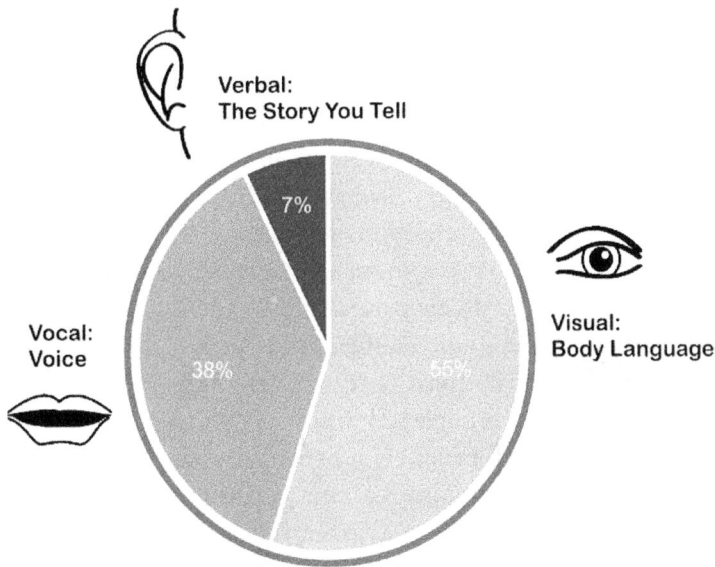

Visual:
Body Language

55%

Body language

Body Language is a kind of nonverbal communication, where thoughts, intentions or feelings are expressed by facial expressions, bodyposture, gestures, eye movement, touch and the use of space. Body language encompasses eye contact, gestures, facial expressions, posture and energy.

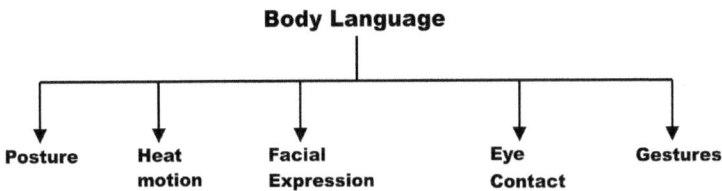

Body Language

| Posture | Heat motion | Facial Expression | Eye Contact | Gestures |

Features of Body Language

There are many ways to keep the audience attention to us, but let us start with our energy!

1. Energy

People often begin their presentations with a greeting, mostly "Good Morning!" with modesty and a polite smile and sometimes nervousness writ large on their face and understandably so. But on very few occasions have I witnessed people saying "Good Morning" and meaning it!! What do I mean? When it's a good morning, it is a good thing to be upbeat about it rather than muttering a nervous greeting.

We need to focus on our energy – get it upbeat and positive! We have to remember to keep our anxieties away for the moments when we are greeting our potential listeners!

What we can do here is to practise saying the greeting a little 'bigger' than we normally would. It will take us out of our comfort zone but with practice, it becomes easier and our comfort zone grows! Initially you may feel that you are shouting but getting a little bigger is not shouting – rather it is a more happy confident you – as perceived by the audience.

It helps to remember happy incidents in our life; for example, when we were with a best friend, animatedly chatting away and being demonstrative with our gestures. If it puts a smile on our face, then it certainly was a correct thing to do. And that is exactly the intensity and energy; we would require during our presentation / speech to bring out our passion for the subject matter.

Remember – don't hold back. It works in our favour to be a wee bit bigger with our gestures and a tad louder with our voices. When we show passion, the audience understands our passion and it will rub off on them too, positively.

2. Voice and Intonation

It's not what we say but how we say it! Listeners listen not just to our words but they can discern our emotions behind the words. You must have come across the phrase in some novels "She heard the smile in his voice!" That means that the listeners read our tone and listened to the words. When the two go hand-in-hand, we look credible.

Voice intonation is all expanding our pace and range of voice, vertically and horizontally, for clarity. It is about getting louder and getting smaller with our volume to bring variety in our speech and avoid being monotonous (vertical range). It is about speeding up and slowing down, developing both ends of the range for impact.

We can practise-play with our voice. For example, there is a word "enthusiastic" in our speech and we say it flatly in a normal tone, the audience is not going to feel the enthusiasm. However, when we get into the meaning of the word and say it energetically and emphatically, the audience will be persuaded!! It is about emphasizing certain words for impact.

As an example, try saying the bold words with emphasis and others in a normal tone. The same sentence then would carry different meanings depending on which word is more emphatic than others.

I *didn't* say he took my money.

I didn't say *he* took my money.

The emphasis on a certain word draws the listener's attention to that word and the speech is transformed when we practise this for certain words throughout our speech.

An emphatic tone of voice sometimes can be perceived as aggression. Smiling will help you to become assertive and emphatic at the same time as smiling takes away the aggression.

3. *Gestures*

I have often seen many speakers using their hands and some others struggling to use their hands when they are speaking, not knowing what to do with the hands. The answer is we use them. According to body language experts Allan & Barbara Pease, "Using hands gestures grabs attention, increases the impact of communication, and helps individuals (in audience) retain more of the information they are hearing."

Gestures are a part of our everyday lives. We wave, point, signal and use our hands when we're speaking animatedly. We express ourselves through gestures,in tandem with our words, often without thinking.

In a speech or presentation situation, we can use gestures effectively and look very natural at the same time. There are some positions of hands which are a complete NO – hands clasped together and held in front of your body, hands behind your back, hands in pockets, hands holding a pen or pencil as a comfort crutch! This positioning of hands can make a speaker come across as defensive, casual and stiff. The best way is to keep the hands away from each other and away from your body, in an open and free manner. Then you will be able to use them easily to enhance your words. With practice and more practice, you will be able to make your gestures align with your words.

Another question which troubles some of our speaker friends is - they are told by some colleagues that they use their hands way too much! Actually there is nothing like less or more when you are gesturing. All feedback that you get may not always be constructive. So the better way is to use your hands and show your energy.

Gestures can be bigger or smaller, but never less or more. When we do small gestures, we do them because we are comfortable with them. These may work in a boardroom kind of setting. However, when your audience is a big group, smaller gestures are lost on them. It is the time to get bigger with your hand movements and louder with your voice to engage people with you and stop them from being on their cell phones or yawning.

The meaning of gestures can be very different across cultures and regions, so it's important to be careful to avoid misinterpretation.

4. Eye Contact

Human beings are very visual folks. Since the visual sense is dominant for most people, eye contact is an especially important type of nonverbal communication. The way you look at someone can communicate many things, including interest, affection, hostility, or attraction.

Eye contact is important in maintaining the flow of conversation and for gauging the other person's response. Speakers who maintain consistent eye contact with their audiences are more effective than those who don't. Clearly, it is not easy to keep consistent eye contact, but at the same time it is not good to pick out one person from the audience and continue to look at them only. A fair approach is to look at the audience from your right to your left, holding the gaze of an audience member for about 2-3 seconds. It is not possible to count seconds whilst we are talking. Ideally move your gaze to a person sitting 2 places ahead after 3-4 words. This way you keep the eye contact going and also look at more than half the audience members.

5. Posture

This type of nonverbal communication includes your bearing, stance and subtle movements. In your role as a public speaker, everything about your physical presence should convey to the audience that you feel confident and comfortable being in control of the room. Your posture contributes tremendously to that impression. It is often the main characteristic of a confident personality when creating positive first impressions.

Getting a good posture is to stand upright and avoid slouching and slumping. Square your shoulders with the audience – face them directly.Do not tilt your body at an angle away from them. Angling your body towards a specific portion of the audience works when you are soliciting audience feedback; it can help encourage audience participation.

6. Head Motion and Facial Expression

In oral communication, the movement of the head helps the posture immensely. It is not a good idea to keep shaking your head, but appropriate nods of the head enhance the level of communication.

Face is the index of the mind. However much one tries, the hidden feelings of anger, fear, confusion, uncertainty, enthusiasm and joy will get revealed by the facial expression. It is best to practice composure.

It is possible that during your speech, you may blank out for a very short time. Those small five seconds however feel like two hours when standing up there. But this is the time to look composed and at ease! We need to practise composure at this moment, Look at the audience, smile and pause till it comes back to you and then carry on with poise. No one will ever guess what had just happened. Easier said than done? It is only practice that gets us there.

Some of us get asked questions that we do not like, but we need to answer them anyway. So keep calm, keep smiling and answer with all the humility you can. You will win hearts of the people watching you.

You may have just delivered the world's best presentation or the exact opposite. In both situations, make your Thank You's and walk away with your head high and a smile on your face till you are out of sight! It will be okay to express yourself once you are behind the scenes. This practice goes a long way in handling all types of people – compassionate audience or the Devil's Advocate!! Challenging audiences like media persons, your subordinates, your board members can be won over with practice.

5. A Few Do's & Don'ts

1. When you walk up to give your speech / presentation, try to
    glance over the audience. It is not too difficult to find a few
    kind and smiling faces who encourage you right at the onset.
    It is possible that you may find none. Smile at a few who
    you think will reciprocate and get the mood built in.
    Audiences have all kinds of faces - few are enthusiastic,
    others are nervous and yet few are dull too and many others
    curious! Be positive and stay focussed! Audiences on a whole
    are a responsible lot! When you put them at ease by being
    at ease yourself, things will go smoothly than you can
    possibly imagine.

2. If you are still learning the ropes of being a good speaker,
    then you may want to give out some printed material in
    form of leaflets, handouts or notes. The material should be
    brief without giving away the central theme of your speech.
    You will just spoil the suspense and the fun element by doing
    so!! This actually is a crutch for beginners and it is not a
    very good idea for the following reasons:

    *   Few members of the audience read the notes and put
        their thinking wheels in motion. Chances are – they may
        be the ones to interrupt you in the middle of the speech
        and take control away from you!
    *   There will be others who will be prepared to fire their
        questions at you the moment you finish and you might
        be caught unaware!
    *   Again there is no fun in spoiling the suspense by giving
        away our plan right at the start!

3. Let the first few lines come out with strong voice. Then vary

the voice tone and speed depending on the demanding situation and crux of the subject.

4. Do not memorize your speech / presentation in its entirety. It has its own pitfalls. You may forget a word and it snaps the link to the rest of your content. You are blanked out and recovery in front of an audience waiting for you is never ever easy!

5. Practise your speech / presentation. Ideally practice should be done with a coach, who is a certified professional or expert. If you don't have these means, you can practise by standing in front of a mirror and becoming your own coach.

6. Remove all barriers like stands, desks and lecterns. If you are restricted by a lectern, use your hands in a bigger and wider way and maintain eye contact with the audience. It looks energetic and people will not feel your reservations with the lectern. A great example here is when our Prime Minister, Narendra Modi gives speeches at political rallies. He is up on a stage, with his speech and a podium. And yet, he is energy personified, with his bigger gestures that seem to include the entire audience, his voice that carries over very well and his eye contact sweeping over the entire gamut of listeners! Nothing can stand in his way of him delivering his message!

7. There comes a time in every episode of speaking where audiences support and help you relax. Look forward to this moment.

8. Stay cheerful. This attribute may not be your strong point. But it needs to be acquired for the event. Cheerfulness is inculcated and strengthened with positive outlook, with optimism and affirmation. Sometimes you may be required to be serious. For example, you may be breaking the news to your employees about expected industry restructuring and job losses. Serious faced moments and deliveries have to be short lived enough to give right impact. One should be

careful that serious gestures is a two edged concept; it may swing the audiences either way.

9. Talking too long is not advisable. You may be digging up trouble for yourself! Practise the KISS maxim – Keep It Short and Simple! The average attention span of human beings is a maximum of twenty minutes. If you find that your speech will be longer than that, try to include activities that the members of the audience can carry out. These activities need to be meaningful – they should ideally make the audience understand the point that you are making through your speech. You can vary between using a few activities, interspersed between your talking. However, too many activities can spoil the show!

10. On technical front, use visual aids wherever required such as a chart or a picture on the screen. But do not talk to your visuals!! Don't turn your back to the audience while trying to explain the visual! It is considered downright rude and does not work any favours for your image as a presenter. If you are using a video – don't talk! You have included the video because you want the audience to view it and they want the same. Watch the video with them and when it gets done, you can resume. Audiences like to look at things and listen and your words paint the pictures in their mind.

11. As far as possible, steer clear of talking about religion, politics and sex! Use humour but don't make fun of other people – colleagues, competitors or some famous celebrity. You might end up rubbing some members of the audience in the wrong way. If you want to use jokes – joke on yourself first! Self-deprecation usually works and listeners may become more receptive to your brand of humour! A good example is the Bollywood actor Shahrukh Khan compering the awards show. He always makes fun of himself first and then gets them all in!

12. Small gestures matter. Pointing fingers at the audience can look threatening – use open hands always; walking about with your shoes clanking on the floor is very distracting – move only for a reason; using filler words like "you know…" again and again weaken the impact of the point you are trying to make – do away with all such extra words and practise pausing instead for impact!

13. Generally every speech has three main segments: Opening, Body (main subject matter) and Closing. The end segment influences the audience with your message when you deliver it correctly. Always finish off with a "Thank You" and a smile!

Armed with the above do's and don'ts, let us delve into what makes a good speech / presentation.

6. Openings & Closings

Openings

"The next ten minutes are going to be the most worthwhile reading moments in your life!"

And in these next ten minutes, we are going to learn and understand the importance of an opening in a speech, ways to do it successfully and also what not to do!

The starting point of any speech is the opening and a good opening

- Gets the audience attention towards the speaker
- Gives an insight into the speech topic
- Helps to establish rapport with the audience, in the way it is delivered
- And it is only 5 – 10 % of the entire speech!

The intention of an opening is to grab the audience attention and get them to listen to the rest of the speech with all their attention and curiosity!. The opening is like a newspaper headline – short, sharp and punchy – written to catch our attention and get us to read the newspaper article!

When I opened this topic with an assertive statement, I got your attention and it also gave you – the readers – an idea of what's coming next.

There are different types of openings. Which type of opening is correct type to use depends on –

- What is the context of the speech? and
- Who is the audience?

In order to launch our presentation with originality and verve, there are a fewtools that can be used as speech pegs when you're wondering how to open a speech:

- Story

- Quotation
- Visual
- Statistic
- Startling statement
- Personal anecdote or experience
- Humour
- Expert opinion
- Sound effect
- Testimony or success story

The best speech openers are the best grabbers who engage an audience immediately, both intellectually and emotionally. Interestingly, these same tools can be used to conclude in a way to keep your audience thinking about your message. Coming up with an exciting opener involves some hard work and stimulated thinking on your part. But the rewards more than justify the effort!

For example, Bill Clinton, in a 1993 speech in Memphis to ministers, after he heard himself introduced as "Bishop Clinton"said, "You know, in the last ten months, I've been called a lot of things, but nobody's called me a bishop yet. When I was about nine years old, my beloved and now departed grandmother, who was a very wise woman, looked at me and she said, 'You know, I believe you could be a preacher if you were just a better little boy.'" This illustrates using a personal story with humour.

Here are a few other opening gambits that can capture audience attention:

1. *Making a startling statement:*

For example, in the United States of America, when giving a speech on a medical treatment gone wrong, the speaker opened his speech with a surprising statement saying, "Doctors are approximately nine thousand times more dangerous than gun-owners!". It jolted the audience out of their stupor and got the speaker their attention.

2. *Making an obscure statement:*

We can arouse the curiosity of an audience with an obscure

statement like "Speak when you are angry and you will make the best speech you will ever regret!"

3. A Dramatic Story:

Tell a small story with lots of drama in words and voice tone and you will have the audience on the edge of their seats.

"A weird thing happened to me last night. I was sleeping in my bedroom around 3 am and I heard the TV being switched on. It was weird because I was all alone in my house!!"

4. Using humour objectively:

For example: "When a man opens the car door for his wife, it is either a new car or a new wife!" or

"People say you can't live without love – but I think oxygen is far more important!"

5. Using quotes of famous personalities:

Using quotes of prominent personalities helps us to establish authority in our speech. For example, Mahatma Gandhi has been quoted since time immemorial "Be the change you wish to see in the world!" From an anonymous source, "Life is like photography – you need the negatives to develop!"

6. Asking a rhetorical question:

Opening a speech with a question is a style that has caught the fancy of every other speaker! And unfortunately this style has been over used and over abused! I have watched many budding and experienced speakers fall into this trap time and again and it really infuriates me as to why do people consistently give themselves a bad opening pitch! It makes them uncomfortable and then they hem and haw their way through the speech, boring the listeners to tears!

A speech should never start with a question. Why? There are a couple of reasons:

- You start your speech by asking a question and members of the audience look nervously at each other, not wanting to answer the question, in case they get it wrong. And, no one would like to be the first person to give a wrong answer.

What has just happened is that you have made your audience nervous and you haven't even started as yet!

- You start your speech by asking a question and there is an uncomfortable silence in the room. You haven't even started and already the rapport between the audience and you as a speaker has broken down.
- You start your speech by asking a question and you get the answer that you did not want! You have been wrong-footed and now you are on the wrong track. It does absolutely nothing for your self-confidence and you haven't even started into the subject matter!

A rhetorical question does not require an answer. It is worded in a way that leaves the listeners wondering about what is the answer to the question? For example, "a question that should be answered is 'Is World War 3 a future reality?'" Or a speech on hygiene can begin with "how many of us start our day by brushing our teeth?" And then raise our hand to indicate to the audience that a silent response is the answer.

I have been privileged to watch many new speakers as a part of my work. And I have heard quite a few gems of wisdom. Here are a few priceless ones – both known and unknown:

- There are no limits to the sky because there are footprints on the moon.
- Uniqueness is important in a life full of similarities.
- There are two types of people in the world – the givers and the takers. The takers may eat better, but the givers sleep well.
- The only thing harder than walking away is not looking back.
- I may not be where I need to be. Thank God! I am not where I used to be.
- Coming together is the beginning, staying together is progress and working together is success!
- A goal is a dream with a deadline!
- Team means "Together Everyone Achieves More!"
- Success is a very lonely road and you can go through it only when you start trusting yourself.

- Understanding the question is half the answer!
- Genius is 1% inspiration and 99% perspiration.
- The heights of great men were reached and kept, not by sudden flight, but they, while their companions slept, toiled through the night.
- Without order, there's chaos.
- Discipline is the bridge between goals and achievements!
- Fear fades when facts are faced.
- The marble not yet carved can hold the form of every thought the greatest artist has!
- Resolve to be a master of change rather than a victim of change.
- Always do what is right! This will gratify some people and astonish the rest! – Mark Twain
- No one's head aches when he is comforting another!
- Saying 'NO' from deepest conviction is better and greater than saying 'YES' merely to please, or what is worse, to avoid trouble – Mahatma Gandhi
- Life is no brief candle to me. It is a sort of splendid torch which I have got a hold of for the moment, and I want to make it burn as brightly as possible before handing it on to future generations – George Bernard Shaw
- Do not dwell in the past, do not dream of the future, concentrate the mind on the present moment – Buddha
- There are only two ways to live your life. One is as though nothing is a miracle. The other is as though everything is a miracle – Albert Einstein
- There are always three speeches, for every one you actually gave. The one you practiced, the one you gave, and the one you wish you gave. – *Dale Carnegie*
- Oratory is the power to talk people out of their sober and natural opinions. – Joseph Chatfield
- The success of your presentation will be judged not by the knowledge you send but by what the listener receives. – *Lilly Walters*

- There are only two types of speakers in the world. 1. The nervous and 2. The liars. – *Mark Twain*
- Light travels faster than sound. That's why certain people appear bright until you hear them speak. – Albert Einstein
- A good speech should be like a woman's skirt; long enough to cover the subject and short enough to create interest. – Winston Churchill

Finally the don'ts:

Don't talk about your hard work in preparing because many people will not be interested.

Don't use filler words like"Today I would like to tell you….." or "I am going to tell you…..". Rather, get straight to the point.

It is absolutely okay to memorize your opening because it gets you off to a flying start!

To sign off on openings, "A speech is like a love affair – anyone can start it but it requires lots of skill to end it!"

Closings

A well-made opening has the power to get the speaker the attention of the audience members. However it is the end that the audience most remembers and takes away with them.It is the final chance to get through the audience where a good speaker arouses interest and/or convinces and persuades his view point.

Most speakers tend to summarize the key points in their presentation and then:
- Say "Thank You" and that's the end!
- Call out "Any questions"   OR
- "Feel free to call me for any questions!"

A closing is that part of the speech where the speaker has a last opportunity to complete his objective! It may be to change an opinion or inspire an audience to take an action. A closing should have a positive, upbeat impact on the audience. When it is delivered correctly with gestures and voice, it can leave a lasting impression on the minds of the listeners.

There are many ways to create a closing impact on the minds of the audience. Be it a quotable quote, an anecdote, mind boggling statistics, a miraculous story or head spinning disappointment. These techniques can make the end message linger in the minds of audience for a long time.

A few examples:

- On the subject of Environment – My dear listeners, if you are looking forward to leave a beautiful tomorrow where your next generation feel proud of you for having been caring for the nature, then spare yourself at this very moment and take a vow.

- On importance of Village Panchayats - The success of the village panchayats shall depend on their readiness not only to help themselves but also on their readiness to tax themselves.

  We can practice different closings that synchronize with our openings and our messages in our speeches.

- Referring back to the opening and tweaking it to make the closing, works as a summary of what the audience have been through in a nutshell. For example, "We have arrived now, where we began."

- Use a relevant quotation / phrase such as "To sell or not sell was the question. Now we have the answers!"

- Dramatize with a famous movie dialogue and twist it slightly to make it fit to your message.

- A congratulatory close appeals to the audience on a personal level. For example, "Aditya...Hrishikesh...Vaishali...I salute you and everyone in your team and I look forward to your continued success!"

- Challenge the audience by asking them to act now, such as "Let's turn from spectators to participants....."

- Deliver an inspirational statement like "Well done is better than well said. So let's do it!"

- Pull their heart strings and make a lasting emotional appeal. For example, "At the end of your life, you will never regret not having passed one more test, not winning one more verdict or not closing one more deal. You will regret time not spent with a spouse, a friend, a child, or a parent!"

Last but not the least: many people are unwilling to offer an explicit and obvious "call to action" at the end of their speeches. Many speakers feel uncomfortable telling the audience precisely what they want them to do after their speeches end!

People are uncomfortable about coming across as an overly aggressive speaker. Yet there are others who claim that they don't *need* to tell the audience what to do at the end of the speech, because they are confident that the audience will be able to *deduce* what they should do next. It is a mistake to assume as such!

In today's world, where an average person is bombarded with around 500 – 800 emails and messages per day, do you really think that they will pick out only your message to reply back to? If you don't tell people *exactly* what you want them to do, you can very safely assume that they won't do it. You can lose out to competition if you insist on being very subtle.

For example, a young senior manager comes up with a ground-breaking idea to step into new markets and make the company's position strong in those markets. He / she make a strong presentation case to the decision-makers and now it is time to close on a high note. Two scenarios can happen:

- If the employee simply summarizes and ends, what did he do the presentation pitch for?
- However if he gives a call to action at the end, asking the decision-makers to approve of a budget with a ballpark figure or invest in new markets, chances are he would be seen as a visionary who has the foresight to keep the company's bottom line in an increasing trend!

A call to action close can be given to any type of audience who can take the action required from them! For example, our Prime Minister's clarion call for 'Clean India' engaged people from all walks of life to act upon the call.

A good presentation is the result of knowledge, hard work, practice and energy. When all the elements are combined together, great orators are born!!

7. The Subject

Structuring the Speech

Most good writing, we are told, must be structured. A good speech is no exception. Organizing or giving a structure to your speech is very important because

- It helps to improve clarity of thought in a systematic way, for both the speaker and the listener.
- The speech becomes effective as the audiences are able to comprehend the speech and possibly think that the speaker is trustworthy, reliable and credible.

Ideally speeches are organized into three main parts: introduction with opening, middle body comprising the subject matter, summary and conclusion and / or closing.

- Opening – The first thirty seconds of your speech are probably the most important. That is the period of time when you grab the attention of your audience, and engage their interest in what you have to say in your speech. We have seen various strategies and examples on this in the earlier chapter. Now that you have won the attention of the audience, your speech should move effortlessly to the middle of your speech.
- Middle Body – The body of your speech will always be the largest part of your speech. At this point, your audience is prepared to hear your arguments, your thoughts and your opinions on the subject matter of your speech.The best way to set out the body of your speech is by formulating a series of main points that you would want to talk to the audience about.The main points should be organized to give your speech a logical progression, and make the job of the listening an easier one.

- Summary - Summarize the main points of your speech
- Closing – The closing of your speech must contain your strongest material because it becomes the takeaway message for the audience.

The Body – SubjectMatter

The body is a logical pattern of your thoughts about certain ideas, events, objects and processes. Setting a structure to your main body of the speech implies

- Breaking up your content into smaller main points. Each main point constitutes a key-point. Your key-points can be your Unique Selling Points (USPs), claims, features, facts, or lesson parts. The main points are complete sentences that are used to create a dialogue with the audience. You may have a sequence of main points that now make up the entire content you are going to talk about.
- It is now time to logically group together similar main points and link them through transitions. Transitions help the audience to understand the logic and flow happening between the main points.
- Each main point covers an idea, a fact, a feature or knowledge. It is necessary to support this main point with proof (evidence) that you may have about the idea, fact, feature or knowledge. By giving evidence, you build credibility and trust with the audience. Then the main point is summed up by having a transition to the next main point. Transition serves as marker to new main points. Examples of transition: 'As a result, what we have today is.....' or 'If we don't take care of the problem, then.....'
- This continues till you have covered most of the content. At this point, it is necessary to read through the speech that you have prepared and you might want to make some changes to the words used, add a few things, delete something that make not make any sense at that point in your speech.
- What you have now is a structure sandwich! Each main

point that you want to convey as a speaker takes the form of 'Main point – Evidence – Transition' template.

The overall structure of your speech can be summarized as shown below:

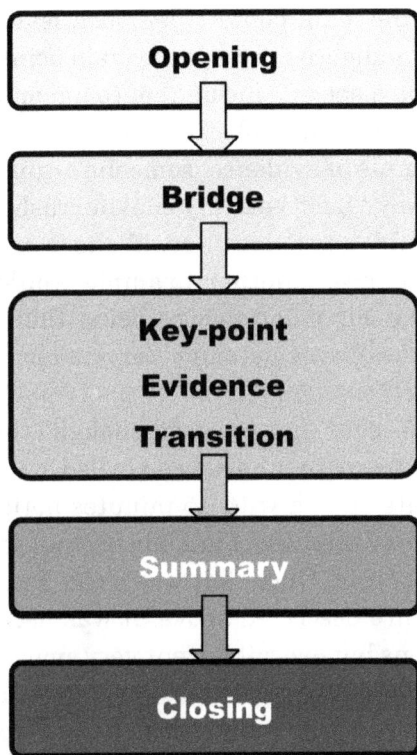

```
┌─────────────────────────┐
│        Opening          │
└─────────────────────────┘
            ⇩
┌─────────────────────────┐
│        Bridge           │
└─────────────────────────┘
            ⇩
┌─────────────────────────┐
│       Key-point         │
│       Evidence          │
│      Transition         │
└─────────────────────────┘
            ⇩
┌─────────────────────────┐
│        Summary          │
└─────────────────────────┘
            ⇩
┌─────────────────────────┐
│        Closing          │
└─────────────────────────┘
```

It is always better to have fewer main points in the body of the speech. Remember we talked about the average attention span of a human being is only twenty minutes. When we curtail our speech to around fifteen minutes, it gives us a breather to add in an important something that may have come up through audience perception. For short speeches, under seven minutes, there should be no more than three main key-points. For longer speeches, more than five main key-points will ensure that audience will have trouble following and remembering the speech. Additionally, you may want to number the main points—first, second, third. Always make it easy for the audience to recognize and follow the main points.

The important trust-building feature of this structure sandwich is the evidence / proof. Evidence serves as confirmation and support for the main points (idea, fact, feature, knowledge) and compels the audience to accept the main points as being true. The proofs can be a specific incident of common knowledge, or a statistic, or a testimonial in black-n-white.

As an example of evidence, someone arguing against seat belt use might say "Last year my cousin crashed her car off a bridge and would have drowned if she were wearing her seatbelt" as evidence. Another example would be, a person talking about the customer service being their USP may say "We have won the Best Customer Service award for the fifth consecutive year!"

Writing speeches that are good-enough is simple and easy when you use a structure. I have been called a couple of times to deliver a 5 minute speech with 15 minutes notice. The hardest part was to think of what can I talk about, that will add value to the current discussion. Once that was clear, I wrote the speech using the structure described above. It was necessary to ad-lib and use quotations but overall it went very smoothly. Obviously, everyone would prefer more preparation, but we are often called upon to "say a few words" on short notice at work or at social events. The structure helps us to do that with ease and comfortably.

This requires practice and with enough practice, the model will stick in firmly in your mind. As you frame your thoughts, you will fill in the blanks, with words. As you deliver the speech, it will flow magically, like watching a movie.

8. The Subject Continued...

Listening, Speaking, Reading and Writing are the four major steps to attain ultimate skill and proficiency in any language. The more developed the listening and reading is, the more prosperous become the facets of speaking and writing. The sequence should normally be: understand a subject, read more of that subject and finally pen down your views on that subject. And then success is guaranteed.

Taking pride in one's own mother language is absolutely natural. But English is a language for wide contacts and public relations. One cannot afford to shy away from it. The voluminous data and the knowledge that is coming out in an explosive way through computers and other media is amazing. Never before was the need felt as it is today, of having good communicators to make this knowledge reach to the masses.

Some examples:

The present world needs communicators like late Professor Ram Shewalkar and alike who had taken up the challenge to take across to the masses, the ever rich themes from Dnyaneshwari!

Lecturing his speech–writers on the value of brevity in a speech, President Lyndon Johnson provided insight into the calibre of a speaker. He said, "Four! That is what I want you to remember. If you do not get your idea across in the first four minutes, you will not do it. Four sentences to a paragraph, four letters to a word. The most important words in the English language all have four letters. Land, Home, Food, Love, Peace..... I know peace has five letters, but any damn fool knows it should have four!"

A speaker should grow in the chosen field like a lobster developing and shedding a series of hard, protective shells. Each time it expands from within, the confining shell gets dropped off. With each event of speaking occasion, a careerist speaker is expected to stretch himself / herself in ways that he or she had not known before. The more a speaker gets exposed, the better the icing cover he or she earns on the oratory form.

A Sr. and the Jr. Pit became famous in history as Master Orators for the pains and sincere efforts both of them had opted to undergo. It was a preparation par excellence, like translating Roman and Greek speeches in their own language, making by heart the innumerable passages from Shakespeare's writings. The effort track went on for years with no break. No wonder their efforts gave them the desired results. Jr. Pit made A 'Wealth of Nation' book by Smith, a tonic to be swallowed for regular consumption. He read all such writings once, twice and wrote them in his own form, paid attention to the construction of sentences, usage of words, its style. Pits and the like ones did all that collection of word wealth, knowledge richness, adoption of speech styles, and last but not the least,took pains to get requisite voice modulation to master the art of speaking.

A speech that leaves a deep impact calls for a lot of perpetual home work. This home work includes becoming jack of all subjects including that of Philosophy, Grammar, Political Science, earning knowledge about local and international laws, religion, traditions, good vocabulary – it's original root analysis, knowing about human nature – it's psychology, dramatic reading of ancient literature. These many are the bare essentials of one's home work. There is another sect of people who differ poles apart on these requisites and advocates that such home work is impossible, as the spectrum of varied subjects under the earth is amazingly very large. And hence they acquaint themselves with a particular and / or few subjects and develop the oratory skills within that given periphery.

In the Indian context, one can say with adequate reasoning that those who made their lives idealistic with what they perceive to be the most appropriate have turned out to be good speakers. This only suggests that those who fight for a cause or those who have taken the noble mission for the life have emerged as good orators, having long lasting impact. Thus one of the qualities though may not be a must, to be a good speaker, is to have dedication. A dedicated mind has always something concrete to offer and hence a single word or couple of words or sentences pronounced by them carries the weight that par exceeds the long drawn speech of a Pundit. The words "Sisters and Brothers of America"of Swami Vivekananda at Chicago meet! Scarcely had he uttered these words when the whole audience was caught up in a great wave of enthusiasm and hundreds rose to their feet with deafening shouts of applause. For the next full two minutes he attempted to speak, but the wild enthusiasm of the audience created by his pure and sacred form of address prevented him from speaking. After silence was restored, he said, "It fills my heart with joy, unspeakable to rise in response to the warm and cordial welcome which you have given us. I thank you in the name of most ancient order of monks in the world; I thank you in the name of the mother of religions; and I thank you in the name of the millions of Hindu people of all classes and sects!"

"We believe not only in universal toleration," said Swami Vivekananda; "but we accept all religions as true. I am proud to belong to a nation which has sheltered the persecuted and the refugees of all religions and all nations of the earth." And he ended by saying, "I fervently hope that the bell that tolled this morning in honour of this convention may be the death knell of all persecution with the sword or with the pen, and of all uncharitable feelings, between persons wending their way to the same goal!"

The Queen of Jhansi, pronouncing the history famous words, 'Meri Jhansi Nahi Dungi' (I will not give up my Jhansi!) can still earn the inspiration that a long drawn speech cannot!

Since the beginning of 20th century till almost independence, the patriots and acclaimed scholars including those thoughtful speakers received and commanded highest respect in the society. Amongst those not possessing the requisite speaking skills remain passive and without recognition. Today speaking skills are hired and paid for. Wealth appeared to have taken an edge over wisdom!! In southern states a new class of professionals in the form of political speakers is emerging. Good professional speakers capable of winning over the audience can earn as much as Rs. 500/- to Rs. 2000/- per public meeting. In state of Tamil Nadu, in one day, professionals manage to be called for 20 to 25 meetings during elections. They have a major role to play. They draw crowds before the leaders make their appearance on the platform. Different speakers use different approaches to hold the attention of masses. Humour, Songs, Poetry Couplets are some of the devices in use to draw more applause then the mere speeches. In Maharashtra, Shahiri Troops used to do this job in the yesteryears.

Oscar Wilde, a literary person was famous for his small, catching, appealing and apparently opposite meaning statements and/or propositions. In English dictionary, these statements are known as EPIGRAMS. For example:

- When you fall in love with self, it's a beginning of a love story that goes on till death.
- Even a wealthiest person can't buy and bring his past to a moment of present.
- A fiancée becoming a wife is like a caterpillar getting converted back to butterfly.
- There are two tragedies in life, one is not to get what you want and other is to get what you want.

In a similar tone, Albert Einstein once said, 'Not everything that counts can be counted, and not everything that can be counted counts.'

A well-known dramatist Ram Ganesh Gadkari's genius personality was no less capable on this track. For example:

- As long as there exist a purpose to live the life, there is an enjoyment to embrace the death too.
- The greatness emerges out of a dedicated death.
- A beautiful woman's statements are weighed not in the weighing scale of truth but that of beauty.

Many effective speakers have consciously inculcated an attribute of 'EMPATHY' in their communication. Empathy is different than sympathy and is something much more. It is the quality of entering fully, through imagination, into another's feelings. In brief, it implies getting into audience skin, so that one really understand and feel one's pain, fear – or more positively their joy and happiness. The opposite of empathy is invalidation. This occurs in a speech when one expresses a feeling or idea, and the audience contradicts or rejects it. Such rejection could be very stressful in the course of speech. There are some speakers who take pleasure in being free, frank, fearless and deliberately abusive. This could be called a one way sermon but never a speech in the subject context.

The truth is that speech is no sudden miracle or accident. It is a result of a fascinating process of exposure, absorption, experiment and modification of good stuff. Here are some points of good stuff :

1. Sarcastic Wit

It is a great idea to keep a store of sarcasms and know how to use them. Navjyot Singh Siddhu, a veteran cricketer and a Member of Parliament, has mastered the art. Siddhu may not be good at cricket commentary. But he is an interesting personality for our subject matter. He enjoys a rare quality of putting the things across in a subtle but sarcastic way.

A little about 'Siddhuism', a term popularly coined for what spice it is, has certainly made any commentary on a given subject interesting. A budding speaker can borrow a lot from Siddhu's oratory figure.

A few of Siddhuism on cricket for our young readers:
- Statistics are like bikinis – what they reveal is suggestive, what they hide is essential.
- Wickets are like wives.You never know which way they will turn.
- He (the batsman) is like a brooding hen over a China egg.
- The ball went so high that it could have got an airhostess on its way down.
- This team is like bicycles in a cycle stand! One falls and the entire row falls!

- The scoreboard is running faster than an Indian taximeter.
- The Indian team without Sachin is like giving a kiss without a squeeze.
- There is a light at the end of the tunnel for Indian team, but it is that of an incoming train which will run them over.
- Age has been a perfect fire extinguisher for the flaming youth.
- Experience is like a comb that life gives you when you are bald.
- He is as innocent as a freshly laid egg.
- On a wardrobe malfunction he said, "One man's wardrobe is another woman's malfunction. The one function I never miss is a wardrobe malfunction."

2. Humour

It is said that humour is gravity concealed behind the jest. More is often taught by a jest than by the most serious knowledge.

"Pakistan is the place every man should send his mother-in-law,for a month, all expenses paid."– Ian Botham

A dentist to a patient: "Good grief, you have the biggest cavity I have ever seen!" the dentist exclaimed as he examined the man. "The biggest cavity I have ever seen!" The patient, very alarmed, snapped back at the dentist, "You need repeat it." "I did not repeat it," replied the dentist. "That was an echo."

The son of a wealthy father decides to get married as he is to inherit a fortune when his ailing widowed father would die. He approaches a beautiful lady and says to her, 'I might be an ordinary looking man, but just in couple of weeks maximum, my father will die and I will inherit billions. Marry me.' The lady went along with him at his home.The next day, she announced that she has become his stepmother.... Ha. Ha.

The pope was on his visit to the US. He suddenly had the strong urge to drive. He told driver so. The driver being a true Catholic did not think of questioning the pope's authority. Thus pope took charge of the wheel and driver got into back seat. They were traveling down the road with an highest possible speed, when policeman happened to see them. He pulled them over and called headquarters reporting a speedy limousine with a VIP inside it. The Chief asked "Who is in the limo? Mayor, Governor or President?" The policeman answered "No someone more important than all these." "Who could be important than these VIPs?"asked the chief in anger. The policeman answered in whispering tone "Sir, I don't know who is this guy, but he has the pope as his chauffeur!"

3. Anecdotes

Short account of interesting tales proves essential for a good speech.

There were three drunkards. They had a party. Drinks were flowing. Ultimately they were left with the last bottle of drink. They decided to share the contents of that left out bottle into three equal parts but only on the next day. Having made up their minds, they went off for sleep. Two of them woke up in the morning and found that the bottle was already empty. They saw the third person lying still in an intoxicated state and so they questioned him. 'Did you empty the bottle? He replied, 'I had only my share.''But you seem to have emptied the entire bottle!' He explained, 'Look, my share was at the bottom of the bottle. To reach there I had to go through your share. And it was gratifying indeed!'

A man had seven daughters. He was facing lots of hardships to feed them and raise them. And now that his daughters were grown up, it was time to find eligible grooms for them and get them married. The man was unhappy for his poor state of affairs. He longed for his peace of mind. He found a saint who could help him find peace. But the saint was to answer only one question. How can I experience joy? This is what I am going to ask him, he said to himself. He approached the saint. The saint was charming young person of marriageable age. On seeing the saint the man could not help but ask, Are you married? The saint replied, No. And then the saint told the man that he cannot ask another question. The man was anxious to find the match for his daughters. Therefore the question just popped out and in process he forgot to ask the right question. The man returned home lamenting.

A man was crying at a rich person's grave. A passer by asked him, Was that rich man a relative of yours ? No, He said. If he was not your relative, then why are you crying for him ? If he had been my relative, he would have a left a lot wealth and huge property for me. And that is the reason I am crying.

A beggar was asking for alms on one of the busy streets. 'Help the destitute, please help....' A motorist halted at the signal and asked him, Why are you begging when you look absolutely fine and fit ? And why do you call yourself destitute? The beggar replied, I am destitute because of my sheer habit of begging that I have developed since I was small.

A person once happened to visit forest where he saw a fox whose leg was broken. He felt sad on seeing the pitiable condition of the fox and started wondering as to how the fox would provide for itself. He then saw the lion coming there with a kill. The lion had its fill and then left the remainder for the fox to feast upon. The person was happy to note that God has made sure that even a lame fox gets food. He muttered to himself, I have no reason to worry. I shall go and sit below the tree and God shall provide me with food. Two days passed and he was still under the tree in a hungry state. O God! I trusted you. You provided for the fox but kept me without food. Suddenly a voice from the sky answered, "You are fit like a lion, copy the lion and not the fox."

I heard this story from an Ex. Vice Chancellor of a famous university. I remember she spoke on a very serious subject. The whole of her speech was mind boggling. But this pathetic story told a lot. The speech became the history for it's more than the desired impact on the audiences. The story was:

God created a four legged animal and said" You will work tireless from sun up to sun down, carrying heavy load on your back, you will not have intelligence, you will eat grass and you will live 50 years. You will be termed DONKEY!" The donkey reacted saying "living 50 years is too much, give me only 20 years." God okayed the proposal.

The next time, God created a barking animal and told him "You will look after a man's home, you will guard his home, you will be his best friend, you will eat whatever is given to you and you will live 25 years. You will be called DOG!" Dog said, "O God! A whole life of 25 years is pretty long. 15 years shall suffice." God gave him 15 years.

God was in happy mood. God created MONKEY and briefed him "You will be an amusing creature, you will do silly things, you will jump from branch to branch and you will live 20 years." Monkey responded saying, "10 years are enough for fun making!" to which God agreed.

Finally God created man, made him sit close by and said, "You will be a man, the only rational being on earth! You will have intelligence, you will control, you will preserve other animals and the surrounding nature, you will dominate the world and you will live for 20 years." Man was unhappy. He pleaded to God, "I will be a man, super in power and living for 20 years is too short. Why don't you give me the 30 years that the donkey refused, the 20 years that the dog did not want and the 10 years that monkey sacrificed?"

That was what God did. And since then, Man lives 20 years like a man, then he enters adulthood and spend 30 years like a donkey working and carrying the load of responsibilities on his shoulder, then when his children leave him and set their homes, he spend 15 years like a dog looking after the house and eating whatever is offered to him. Ultimately he gets into retirement and spends 10 years like a monkey jumping from house to house, from one son to another and doing silly things to amuse grandchildren!

Man's life tragedy lies in this story. He had an option of living life king size for twenty years. Well, it was not to be!

4. Poetry

Reciting good poems can have a dramatic effect on your speech. From the manner of saying such poetic words, people will deduce a great deal about your feelings. Poems often give musical effect to the speech.

"The woods are lovely, dark and deep,
But I have promises to keep,

And miles to go before I sleep,
And miles to go before I sleep...

- By Robert Frost

"So many Gods,
So many creeds,
So many paths,
That wind and wind,
While just the art of being kind,
Is all this sad world needs?

- By Ella Wheeler Wilcox

One find a fresh lease of life in introspection of lines idealized as real-It is the strength of poet. It is a poet's gift of imagination. He helps us to see the glory and the freshness of a dream.

Wordsworth penned down a poem about a matter of fact, the ordinary unimaginative man. He is aware only of what he perceives by his senses and sees only the outward aspect of what he sees.

'A primrose by a river's brim
A yellow primrose to him,
And it was nothing more'
For a poet like Wordsworth
" To me the meanest flower that blows can give
Thoughts that do often lie too deep for tears"

5. Wisdom

Wisdom sayings are the salt of a popular speech, a source of interesting information required for every occasion from birth to death. They come in form of Maxims – A must mix in short speeches – It tells a long story short, but it has to have relevance to the subject.

Some pearls of Wisdom:

A friendship founded on business is better than a business founded on friendship! – John D. Rockefeller

Avoid the faults of our nation – Water shares the good or bad qualities of the channels through which it flows and people share that environment in which they are born. Some owe more than others to their nation because there is a more favourable sky in their zenith.

We are born barbarians and only raise ourselves to be above the beast, by our culture. Once upon a time India and Greece could call the rest of the world barbarians.

Character and intellect are the two poles of our capacity; one without the other is but halfway to happiness.

Knowledge and good intentions together guarantee perpetual success. A fine intellect wedded to a wicked will is always an unnatural monster.

Knowledge and courage are the traits of great personality. They bestow immortality. Each is as much as he knows, and the wise can do anything.

Fortune and fame are two friends where the one is fickle and the other is enduring.

Be diligent and intelligent. Diligence promptly executes what intelligence carefully thought through.

Distinction in speech and action! By this one can earn a position in many places and win esteem.

Do not show your wounded figure, for everything will knock up against it.

6. Maxims

It is a general truth or rule of conduct expressed in a sentence.

A few examples:

If you think you are beaten, you are. If you think you dare not, you do not. If you would like to win, but you think you cannot, it is almost a cinch you will not. If you think you will lose, you are lost.

Sow a thought, reap an action; sow an action, reap a habit; sow a habit, reap a character; sow a character, reap a destiny.

He who knows but knows not he knows, he is full, shun him.

The difference between a Russian wedding and a Russian funeral is that at a funeral there is one person not having vodka.

The friendship of the French is like their wine; exquisite, but of short duration.

A blue eye in a Portuguese woman is a mistake of nature – Spanish Saying.

7. *Rhetorical Tricks*

This may be effective at the end of speech. The most common is repetition.

President late John Kennedy's famous address to the people of Berlin had created a great impact with the use of this repetition trick. An interesting piece of it will make the point clear.

"There are many people in the world, who really do not understand, or say they do not understand what is the great issue between the Free World and the Communist World – Let them come to Berlin. There are some who believe that Communism is the way of the future. Let them come to Berlin. And there are even a few who say that it is true that Communism is an evil system but it permits us to make economic progress. Let them come to Berlin". The repetition of 'there are... there are...' and the refrain; let them come to Berlin successfully put the key points across.

9. Famous Talks!

Swami Vivekananda was an inspired seer, born with a mission. As such everything that had come from his soul has deep significance. It is felt that the philosophy of Swami Vivekananda and the ideals for which he lived and worked could be great source of inspiration to the India Youth. Paying his tribute to Swami, the late Prime Minister *Jawaharlal Nehru* said, 'Many of my generations were very powerfully influenced by him, and I think that it would do a great deal of good to the present generation if they also went through Swami Vivekananda's writings and speeches.

To make the selection of one good speech of it; is not an easy task. To make our younger generation take advantage of this fountain of wisdom, of spirit and fire, and to arouse a desire in young readers to study the Swami's thoughts, here we produce the highlights of one from Nehru's published speeches.

"The Future Of India"

This is the ancient land where wisdom made its home before it went into any other country, the same India whose influx of spirituality is represented, as it were, on the material plane, by rolling rivers like oceans, where the eternal Himalayas, rising tier above tier with their snow-caps, look as it were into the very mysteries of heaven. Here is the same India whose soil has been trodden by the feet of the greatest sages that ever lived. Here first sprang up inquiries into the nature of a man, and into the internal world. Here first arose the doctrines of the immortality of the soul, the existence of a supervising God, an immanent God in nature and in man, and here the highest ideals of religion and philosophy have attained their culminating points. This is the land from whence, like the tidal waves, spirituality and philosophy have again and again rushed out and deluged the world, and this is the land from whence once more such tides must proceed in order to bring life and vigour into the decaying races of mankind. It is the same India which has withstood the shocks of centuries, of hundreds of foreign invasions, of hundreds of upheavals of manners and customs. It is the same land which stands firmer than any rock in the world, with it undying vigour, indestructible life. Its life is of the same nature as the soul, without beginning and without end, immortal, and we are the children of such a country.

Many times have I been told that looking into the past only degenerates and leads to nothing, and that we should look to the future. That is true. But out of the past is built the future. Look back, therefore, as far as you can, drink deep of the eternal fountains that are behind, and after that, look forward, much forward and make India brighter, greater, much higher than she ever was.

The one common ground that we have is our sacred traditions, our religion, and upon that we shall have to build. In Europe, political ideas form the national unity. In Asia, religious ideals form the national unity. We know that our religion has certain common grounds, common to all our sects, however varying their conclusions may be, however different their claims be. Within their limitation this religion of ours admits of a marvellous variation, an infinite amount of liberty to think, and live our own lives. Let everyone of this country, understand these life-giving principles of our religion and try to bring out in their lives.

It is only when the body is weak that the germs take possession of it and cause disease. Just so with the national life. It is when the national body is weak that all sorts of disease germs, in the political state of the race or in its social state, in its educational or intellectual state, crowd into the system and produce impurities.

It is culture that withstands shocks, not a simple mass of knowledge. You can put a mass of knowledge into the world, but that will not do it much good. There must come culture into the blood. The only way to bring about the levelling of caste is to appropriate the culture, and the education to all. Therefore, my friends, it is no use fighting among the castes. It will divide us all the more, weaken us all the more and degrade us all the more. The days of exclusive privileges and exclusive claims are gone, should go for ever from the soil of India. The solution is not by bringing down the higher, but by raising the lower up to the level of the higher.

To make a great future of India, the whole secret lies in organization, accumulation of power, co-ordination of wills. Already before my mind rises one of the marvelous verses of the 'Rig-Veda Samhita' which says "Be thou all of one mind, be thou all of one thought, for in the days of yore, the Gods being of one mind were enabled to receive oblations".

There is yet another point I wish to make. Women make big societies in European societies, and make tremendous declarations of woman's power. For the next fifty years, the woman power shall be our keynote for this, our great Mother India.

The whole day mixing with the world, with 'Karma-Kanda', and in the evening sitting down and blowing through your nose! It is all nonsense. What is needed is 'Chittashudhi, purification of the heart. This comes through the worship of the 'Virat-of those all around us. These are all our Gods- men and animals, and the first Gods we have to worship are our own countrymen.

We must have life-building, man-making, character-making assimilation of ideas. If you have assimilated five ideas and made them your life and character, you have more education than any man who has got by heart a whole library. "The ass carrying it load of sandalwood knows only the weight and not the value of sandalwood". If education is identical with information, the libraries are the greater sages in the world, and encyclopaedias are the Rishis. The ideal therefore is that we must have the whole education of our country, spiritual and secular, in our own hands, and it must be on national lines, through national methods, as far as practicable.

Lastly we must enter into the life of every race in India and abroad; we shall have to work to bring this about. "It is the young, the strong, and healthy, of sharp intellect, that will reach the Lord" say the Vedas. This is the time to decide your future-while you possess the energy of youth, not when you are worn out and jaded, but into freshness and vigour of youth. Work, this is the time, for the freshest, the untouched and un smelled flowers alone are to be laid at the feet of the world, and such he receives. Rouse yourselves, therefore, for life is short. There are greater works to be done. A far greater work is this sacrifice of yourselves for the benefit of your race, for the welfare of humanity. Let this be our determination, and may He, the Lord, who comes again and again for the salvation of his own people.

Address of Azim Premji, Chairman, Wipro while accepting the Businessman of the year 2000 award from Business India in Mumbai on Dec 15, 2000.

I am very honoured to accept this prestigious award. I am also proud to acknowledge the tireless efforts put in by the team of professionals in Wipro who have contributed to the success. Even as I accept this award, I am aware of the tremendous responsibility that lies ahead of us as India transitions herself into the new millennium.

It is over 30 years since I joined Wipro. To me, the journey has been challenging, at times gruelling, but at the same time immensely satisfying. What I treasure most about the experience, are the lessons I have learnt along the way. I would like to share few of them. I hope you will find them as useful as I do.

The first lesson is you must always have the courage to think big. A vision that is beyond what seems to be achievable has a tremendous capacity to ignite the collective imagination and passion of your team. It must not be an impossible dream and one must be prepared to work for it with a single – minded dedication. If the vision is powerful enough, it enables you to tap inner strengths, resources and potential that you did not know existed. It can create enthusiasm that is contagious to those working with you and build the resilience to take risks. As someone said, ships are safe in the harbour, but that is not they were designed for. A vision cannot be safe. Strategies must de-risk it.

Second, you must never compromise on fundamental values, no matter what the situation is. It not only leads to success, but also makes success worthwhile. The only way to create an organization based on values is to demonstrate them transparently and walk the talk. All actions with integrity can stand public scrutiny.

Third you must build tremendous self-confidence. It is needed most when things do not look very bright. But if you are convinced you are right, then go ahead and do what you set out to do. Ignore any pessimists you may meet along the way. To my mind, self-confidence is absolutely fundamental to success. If you do not have confidence in yourself, there is no way that you can expect your employees, your customers and your investors to have confidence in you.

Fourth, you must surround yourself with the best of people. Even if you have to acknowledge that some of them may be better than you. An organization itself does not really accomplish anything. Plans do not accomplish anything. Organizations succeed or fail because of the people involved. Look for people who have the capacity to anticipate and see around corners. Also look for people with loyalty, integrity, a high-energy drive, emotional maturity and an overpowering desire to get things done.

Fifth, you must have an obsessive commitment to quality. Customers want more quality for less cost. That is an absolute global truth. One of the greatest contributions of globalization has been demand for higher quality. Quality is absolute pre-requisite for survival, leave alone success. Like integrity, there can be no compromise in quality.

Sixth, you must play to win. Too long, we have suffered from an ideological hangover, which made people feel a little guilty about making profits or succeeding. Playing to win is one of the finest things you can do. Playing to win stretches you and everyone around you. It gives you a new sense of direction and energy.

Playing to win does not mean playing dirty. If you cut corners along the way, you will miss out on the personal satisfaction of winning. Because, winning means reaching the depth of your own potential and utilizing it to its fullest. Ultimately, your only competition is yourself.

Lastly, the most important facilitator of success is the blessing of a force beyond us. We can call it luck, we can call it GOD. As a non – religious person, I attribute much of my success to the 'force beyond me'. Let me illustrate this with a touching storey.

One night, a man had a dream. He dreamt he was walking along the beach with the Lord. Across the sky flashed scenes from his life. For each scene, he saw two sets of footprints in the sand, one belonging to him and the other to the Lord.

When the last scene flashed before him, he looked back at the footprints in the sand. He found that many times along the path of his life there was only one set of footprints. He also noted that it happened at the most difficult and saddest times in his life.

This really disturbed him and he questioned the Lord thus : "Lord, you said that once I decided to follow you, you would walk with me all the way. But I have noticed that during the most troublesome times in my life, there is only one set of footprints. I do not understand why, when I needed you the most, you would leave me."

The Lord smiled and gently replied, "My precious, precious child, I love you and I would never leave you. During your times of trial and suffering, when you see only one set of footprints, I carried you in my arms."

Azim Premji's Speech at IIT Convocation

I am privileged to be with you here today and to share this significant moment of your life. The convocation marks the culmination of all the endless nights you worked through, all the anxieties you have gone through facing one examination after another and all the preparation you have put in, not only to enter this prestigious institution but also to graduate from it successfully. It is no small achievement. Only a handful of the most talented lot in the world have shared this success with you. Let me say that I am very proud of each and everyone of you.

I am little wary about giving you advice – because advice is one thing young people all over the world do not like receiving. I cannot fault you for that. The world does look very different when it is seen with your eyes. You are filled with enthusiasm and are straining at the least to get on with life.

And the world is very different from what it was when I was your age. Never before has the role of technology been so pervasive and so central. The internet has breached all physical borders and connected the world together like no other force has done before. For the first time, opportunities for creating wealth in India are at par with the best of the world. There is no need for you to sacrifice the joy of remaining in your own country any more.

All opportunities are accompanied by their own challenges. I thought I would share with you a few of the lessons I have learnt in my own life, while leading the transformation at WIPRO, from a small company three and half decades back into a global corporation listed on the New York Stock Exchange. I hope you find them useful.

Lesson 1 : Dare to Dream

When I entered WIPRO at the age of 21, it was sudden and unexpected event. I had no warning of what lay ahead of me and I was caught completely unprepared. All I had with me was a dream, a dream of building a great organization. It compensated for my inexperience and I guess, also prevented me from being overwhelmed by the enormity of the task before me.

What I am happy is that we never stopped dreaming, even when we achieved a position of leadership in every business we operated in India. We now have a dream of becoming one of the top 10 global IT service companies.

Many people wonder whether having unrealistic dreams is foolish. My reply to that is dreams by themselves can never be realistic or safe. If they were, they would not be dreams. I do agree that one must have strategies to execute dreams. And of course, one must slog to transform dreams into reality. But dreams come first.

What saddens me most is to see young, bright people getting completely disillusioned by a few initial setbacks and slowly turning cynical and some of them want to migrate to US in the hope this is the solution. It requires courage to keep dreaming. And that is when dreams are most needed – not when everything is going right, but when just about everything is going wrong.

Lesson 2 : Define what you stand for

While success is important, it can become enduring only if its built on a strong foundation of values. Define what you stand for as early as possible and do not compromise with it for any reason. Nobody can enjoy the fruits of success if you have to argue with your conscience.

In WIPRO, we defined our beliefs long before it became a fashion to do so. It not only helped us in becoming more resilient to stand up to crises we faced along the way, but also helped us in attracting the right kind of people. Eventually we realized that our values made eminent business sense. Values help in clarifying what everyone should do or not do in any given situation. It saves enormous time and effort because each issue does not have to be individually debated at length. Also let us remember that values are meaningful only if you practice them. People may listen to what you say but they will believe what you do. Values are a matter of trust. They must be reflected in each one of your actions. Trust takes a long time to build but can be lost quickly by just one inconsistent act.

Lesson 3: Never lose your zest and curiosity

All the available knowledge in the world is accelerating a phenomenal rate. The whole world's codified knowledge base (All documented information in library books and electronic files) doubled every 30 years in the early 20th century. By the 1970s, the world's knowledge base doubled every 7 years. Information researchers predict that by the year 2010, the world's codified knowledge will double every 11 hours. Remaining on top of what you need to know will become one of the greatest challenges for you.The natural zest and curiosity for learning is one of the greatest drivers for keeping updated on knowledge. A child's curiosity is insatiable because every new subject is a thing of wonder and mystery. The same zest is needed to keep learning new things. I personally spend at least 10 hours every week on reading. If I do not do that , I find myself quickly outdated.

Lesson 4 : Always strive for excellence

There is a tremendous difference between being good and being excellent in whatever you do. In the world of tomorrow, just being good is not enough. One of the greatest advantages of globalization is that it has brought in completely different standards. Being the best in the country is not enough; one has to be the best in the world. Excellence is the moving target. One has to constantly raise the bar.

In the knowledge based industry, India has the unique advantage of being a quality leader. Just as Japan was able to win in the overseas market with its quality leadership in automobile manufacturing, India has been able to do the same in information technology. At WIPRO, we treat quality as the number one priority. This enabled us not only to become the world's first SEI CMIM level 5 software services Company but also a leader in Six Sigma approach to quality in India. Doing something excellently has its own intrinsic joy, which I think is the greatest benefit of quality.

Lesson 5 : Build Self Confidence

Self-confidence comes from a positive attitude even in adverse situations. Self-confident people assume responsibility for their mistakes and share credit with their team members. They are able to distinguish between what is in their control and what is not. They do not waste their energies on events that are outside their control and hence they can take setbacks in their stride. Remember, no one can make you feel inferior without your consent.

Lesson 6 : Learn to work in teams

The challenges ahead are so complex that no individual will be able to face them alone. While most of our education is focused in individual strength, teaming with members is equally important. You cannot fire a missile from a canoe. Unless you build a strong network of people with complimentary skills, you will be restricted by your own limitations.

Globalization has brought in people of different origins, different upbringings and different cultures together. Ability to become an integral part of a cross – cultural team will be a must for your success.

Lesson 7 : Take care of yourself

The stress that a young person faces today while beginning his or her career is the same as the last generation faced at the time of retirement. I have myself found that my job has become enormously more complex over the last couple of years. Along with mutual alertness, physical fitness will also assume a great importance in your life.

You must develop your own mechanism for dealing with stress. I have found that a daily job for me, goes a long way in releasing the pressure and building up energy. You will need lots of energy to deal with the challenges. Unless you take care of yourself there is no way you can take of others.

Lesson 8 : Persevere

Finally, no matter what you decide to do in your life, you must preserve, preserve and preserve. Keep at it and you will succeed, no matter how hopeless it seems at times. In the last three and half decades, we have gone through many difficult times. But we have found that if we remain true to what we believe in, we can surmount every difficulty that comes in the way. I remember reading this very touching story on perseverance.

An eight year old child heard her parents talking about her little brother. All she knew was that he was very sick and they had no money left. They were moving to a smaller house because they could not afford to stay in the present house after paying the doctor's bills. Only a very costly surgery could save him now and there was no one to loan them the required money.

When she heard daddy say to her tearful mother with whispered desperation, " Only a miracle can save him know, " the child went to her bedroom and pulled a glass jar from its hiding place in the closet. She poured all the change on the floor and counted it. Clutching the precious jar tightly, she slipped out the back door and made her way six blocks to the local drug store. She took a quarter from a jar and placed it on the glass counter.

"And what do you want ?asked the pharmacist. 'It's for my little brother, the girl answered back. He is really really sick and I want to buy miracle. I beg your pardon! said the pharmacist. My little brother is Andrew and he has something bad growing inside his head and my Dad says only a miracle can save him. So how much does a miracle cost? My dear child, We don't sell miracles here, I am sorry, the pharmacist said, smiling sadly at the little girl.

"Listen, I have the money to pay for it. If it is not enough, I can try and get some more. Just tell me how much it costs." In the shop was a well – dress customer. He stepped down and asked the little girl, 'What kind of a miracle does your brother need? I don't know. She replied with her eyes welling up. He is really sick and mommy says he needs an operation. But my daddy can't pay for it, so I have brought my savings. How much do you have? asked the man. 'One Dollar and Eleven Cents, but I can try and get some more, she answered barely audibly.' "Well what a coincidence " smiled the man. A Dollar and Eleven Cents – the exact price of a miracle for little brother. He took her money in one hand and held her with the other. He said, Take me to where you live, I want to see your little brother and meet your parents. Let's see if I have the kind of miracle you need!

That well – dressed man was Dr. Carlton Armstrong, a surgeon, specializing in neuro – surgery. The operation was completed without charge and it was not long before Andrew was home again and doing well. That surgery, mom whispered, was a real miracle. I wonder how much it would have cost? The little girl smiled. She knew exactly how much the miracle cost; One Dollar and Eleven Cents plus the faith of a little child!!

Lesson 9 : Have broader social vision

For decades we have been waiting for someone who will help us in 'priming the pump' of the economy. The government was logical choice doing it, but it was strapped for resources. Other countries were willing to give us loans and aids but there was a limit to this. In the millennium of the mind, knowledge – based industries like information technology are in a unique position to earn wealth from outside. While earning is important, we must have mechanisms by which we use it for the larger good of the society.

Through the Azim Premji Foundation, we have targeted over the next 12 months to enroll over a million children, who are out of school due to economic or social reasons. I personally believe that the greatest gift one can give to others is the gift of education. We who have been so fortunate to receive this gift know how valuable it is.

Lesson 10 : Never let success go your head

No matter what we achieve, it is important to remember that we owe this success to many factors and people outside us. This will not only help us in keeping our sense of modesty and humility intact but also help us retain our sense of proportion and balance. The moment we allow success to build a feeling of arrogance, we become vulnerable to making bad judgments.

Let me illustrate this with another story:

A lady in faded dress and her husband, dressed in a threadbare suit, walked in without an appointment into the office of the President of the most prestigious educational institution in America. The secretary frowned at them and said, 'He shall be busy all day'. 'We will wait' said the couple quietly.

The secretary ignored them for hours hoping they will go away. But they did not. Finally the secretary decided to disturb the President, hoping they will go away quickly once they meet him.

The President took one look at the faded dress an glared sternly at them. The lady said, 'Our son studied here and he was very happy. A year ago, he was killed in an accident. My husband and I would like to erect a memorial for him in the campus.'

The President was not touched. He said Madam, we cannot put up a statue for every student of ours who died. This place will look like a cemetery. Oh, No! the lady explained quickly, we do not wish to erect a statue, we thought we would give a building to the campus.

Speech of MARK ENGLIS

"Life is not rehearsal, It's the main show and only once, one gets a chance to live and perform, so make most of it." Words pronounced in a debut address, sent spinning but positive waves on the audience as these came from a person who mountaineered the world's highest peak 'Everest' with no human legs.

I am not a Philosopher, neither a scholar nor an acclaimed wise man. Half the century of my life I have spent doing what I felt 'A MUST DO '. I am not known to concede the defeat so easily. Two decades back, I lost both of my legs in a mountaineering expedition. I was working as the Search and Rescue Mountaineer. My job was to rescue those who get trapped. See the destiny, Rescuer that I was, once got totally jammed in a ice cave. Nature made our that particular expedition track irreversible. SOS were sent and the rescuers reached to the concerned bodies right in time. Efforts were made from every nook and corner and also from Government level and on a war footing. Yet it took them 14 days to rescue us. That inordinate time has taken its toll of victims. My ice cold legs went numb and lost total sensation, end result had to acupuncture from knees. My legs were my bread and butter. 24 years have elapsed since ..... that trage event.

During this testing time, I earned a degree in Human Bio Chemistry with distinction. I learnt making wine at home later on to become the leading Wine Maker of my country 'NewZeland'. I introduced series of ready made healthy food and recipes to make them. I convinced the people that life is too small to go without quality healthy food. This message earned a brand name for my food products.

Skiing was my passion, I continued that with greater zeal. I could succeed in bringing handicap persons closer and comfortable to the skiing adventure sport. Cycling was my childhood hobby. Artificial legs did not deter me from taking long ride on cycles. I could earn a medal in cycling event at 2000 Sydney Paralympics .

My adverse and rich experiences gave me adequate courage for writing. I developed a flair for writing. My writings started getting wide acceptance across the country. Invitations started pouring from my fellow countrymen to share my experiences. In the year 2003, in a road show that became popular by name 'In Zone' I got the privilege to meet 60000 students from across the country. An ordinary person that I was; became an all country figure. Sharing further, multiplied my zeal to work hard. The stones of hurdle..... I converted them into steps to reach greater heights. A new path emerged in the process. Limitations did not stand in my way. I dreamt big and galloped to make them a stark reality. I moulded my personality open for adoptions.

To reach Everest was one such dream I ever cherished in my heart. I had no human legs made; full of life. A call from mountains was knocking my heart. In January 2002, I rested my foot on Oraki on the Mount Cook range of mountains. My country bestowed on me the Order of Merit. On 27th September 2004, I succeeded in putting my foot on a peak known as Cho Oyu. It was on a altitude of 8201 meters. History recorded the achievement of capturing of a peak of that altitude by a leg less person. Your legs whether they are made up of flesh and bones or Carbon Titanium.... Does that really matter ? What's significant is your dual engine a mind and body ! How you make that engine support your ideas?

To quote Earnest Hemingway, Mountaineering is a game which only knows 'possible or not possible' A single lapse or small mistake may take you to grave. 'I take my onward journey to reach the destined peak'...........a positive statement one has to sign for oneself. That is a *'mantra'* There is nothing like, Try. No ifs and buts!

On that positive note and chanting that 'mantra' I proceeded to conquer the highest challenging peak of Himalayas, the king of peaks 'Everest'. On a lower base camp, cold caught my throat. At Lahsa, right stump got wounded. Rest of my team went in for practice leaving me at camp. Everest expedition gave me the first indication, Get ready for a tougher track, you leg-less fellow!! This is how I interpreted it. Nature as you move up; is never friendly. It spreads a larger canvass of dangers and unpredictability. Stomach upset, sun burns to wounded stumps, all the privileged sufferings I went through. Rest and start again became my routine. This circle kept repeating, but I never gave up. My determination went stronger each time such problems cropped up. To add icing to the cake of problems, ice storms came our way with greater frequency. I felt Himalaya was discouraging me to embrace its peak Everest.

At last, after sustaining all that pleasure troubles, I could reach the destined peak on 15th May 2006. It took me 40 days. Leg less fellow that I was reached on top of the world. I gathered a feeling that Mount Everest patted me on my back. Happiness mounted.

'Legs for all' is my next dream. I have a message to all handicapped, 'Give me your strong will' I will make your journey affordable. Nature is cruel in mountains is one statement, but all Marks' with strong will can still conquer it, is another statement.

Mark's speech was full of life. The impact of his speech made the pack of audience totally speechless.

10. Some Speeches

As a member of RSS, I had few privileges to give a talk before the small and committed group. I also got good opportunities to speak during my college functions. In my corporate span of two decades too, I have snatched umpteen occasions to speak before the learned lot. The following three talks, I felt I was at my best. Later two of those talks got duly published as center columns in one of the leading newspapers of Pune.

Speech 1

My brothers,

I must admit that I am the most worried person today by the disturbing course of events we all have witnessed during the last fortnight or so.

In days to come, Ram Setu could be the issue that may give an impetus to the RSS nationalists. And that the RSS should really pick it up as a cultural cum geo-archaeological issue; and why not if the news is true to its core about the Central Government unceremoniously deciding to pull down the said Ram Setu. Every effort should be made to bring the awareness among the people and thereby force the government to abandon its evil plans in that direction.

V Sundaram, an IAS officer and one who played a major role in commissioning of Tuticorin Harbour Project in his capacity as its Chairman, has noted that the Ram Setu bridge acted as a natural barrier in preventing the direct devastation of the entire southern coastline during the last tsunami in December 2004.

The reports of experts tracing a lost city beneath Alexandria that was flourishing around 1000 BC, should serve as an inspiration for Indian minds to get to the heart of the Ram Setu issue.

Ram Setu was known to have built by the then king of Ayodhya, Lord Rama. Let me narrate the events that led to building of the said Setu. As you all know Rama takes the path of vanvas in order to follow and execute the promise given by his father Dashratha to Kaikayee. He relinquishes the Rajdharma and leaves the kingdom for fourteen years of vanvas to fulfill that promise. Dharmapatni Sita and brother Laxman vow to accompany Rama during those testing period of fourteen years. While in vanvas the demon king Ravana of Sri Lanka treacherously takes away Sita to his kingdom and holds her in captivity surrounded by guards. The epic Ramayana further describes that Rama with the help of monkey army builds up a bridge (Ram Setu) across the Rameshwaram and Jaffna to reach Sri Lanka. He fights a war with Ravana and succeeds in getting back Sita. The return journey from Sri Lanka to Ayodhya was made using the mythical Pushpak Yan (Air craft) belonging to the kingdom of Ravana. This is a brief series of events. Every Hindu has been hearing and chanting this epic story in various forms for thousands of years. This story is based on fervent belief that it is beyond challenge.

Since then however, the said Ram Setu vanished and was said to have submerged under the sea. When and how are questions best left to the historians. But to trace back its existence is a matter of national pride and a challenge to present day navigators and coastal geo-archaeologists of that field. I feel further research could shed light on the use of the bridges of those times. And then this cultural issue can get converted into a science subject, as today virtually nothing is known of the marine army who built that Ram Setu, if indeed humans had built it.

The Ramayana written by Valmiki around 200 BC, throws ample light on the chapters of war fought by Rama, the path and the journey of his efforts in that direction. However it is the great poet Kalidas who encompasses in the 13 sarga of his poetic creation Raghuvansha the most authentic description of Rama building the Ram Setu and the onward events of war and his return journey.

Let me share one interesting story of efforts taken up by one Dr. S.V.Bhave of Pune. He was from a medical fraternity and he was an amateur and enthusiast pilot. He was highly impressed and influenced by Kalidasa's Raghuvansha. He had taken up the challenge and had actually undertaken a journey to and from Sri Lanka by his own aircraft. In that noble endeavour he came out with lot of evidence to conclude the existence of Ram Setu. He further published his book in Marathi on the thrilling journey he had undertaken for the cause. In that book he has exhibited a picture of him actually standing four feet deep on the said lost bridge. Curious readers would really enjoy reading of that book.

On Vijayadashmi day, Dr. Bhave put all out efforts and marched his journey on a path described by Kalidasa 1600 years ago. He traced down the Akashganga (Milky Way) appearing during the then time, and went ahead with the assumption that underneath he should find the traces of Ram Setu. He observed on that particular day, the track of Akashganga was passing through the lines of Kanyakumari, Trivendram and that of Malay range of mountains. With that imaginary line he could visualize the extended axis joining the south and north pole and that comes from the earth planet and from where he could sight the Dhruva star. He underlined his observation that the earth rotates around this very axis and around itself. As we know, Dr. Bhave too knew that the subject axis does not remain in one direction as its north end rotates in one circle and gradually its speed of rotating reduces. 13000 years back the subject axis was pointing towards the Vega star and the axis was to complete 360 degree rotation in 26000 years. Thus after 26000 years its end should point the Solaris or Dhruva star. He had studied the concept of Precession of Equinox which stated that the said axis rotates only one degree in 72 years. Taking into consideration this basic home work Dr.Bhave tried to find out as to where could the Akashganga that he could see on this day of his journey at 5.30 am would have been when Kalidasa wrote the related chapters? By simple calculations, 1600 divided by 72 gives a degree of 22.2. If the extended axis is fixed up on Malay range of mountains and rotated by 22.2 degree to the east of Kanyakumari, should be the place of Akashganga and underneath Ram Setu. Dr. Bhave not satisfied with his own mathematics had this premise checked and verified from renowned professor of Physics. The observations and the facts were put on the map and he painstakingly followed the track by boat and to his joy and to the joy of proud Indians, he found the Ram Setu.

The recent space images captured by NASA reveal a mysterious ancient bridge in the Palk Straits between India and Sri Lanka. Thank GOD, NASA unlike our politicians was not influenced by any vested interests to reveal the results.

At present, the connecting sea in between the two nations India and Sri Lanka has been recorded as historical waters under the international norms and as such both the countries enjoy a de facto ownership over it. The most talked about Setu – Samudram project if implemented shall pave a way for an international boundary open for trafficking on the high seas. The other argument against the implementation of the Setu – Samudram project put forth is we may loose the rich Thorium deposits. And Thorium is known to be an essential ingredient of next generation nuclear power.

Thanks for a peaceful listening.

Jai Hind.

Speech 2

My Brothers,

I have the pleasure to welcome you all to this solemn function. The Jan Jagran Samiti considers it an honor to host this function organized to felicitate the revered Gurujans who grace this dais today. I must nevertheless state that this felicitation of the revered Gurujans present on this dais today is in their capacity as representatives of the teaching community at large and also that is best, noble and sacred in our great tradition of the Guru - Shishya concept, as well as India's rich history in the field of learning and education. The revered personalities on the dais shall shortly enlighten us in depth on the many different facets of learning and education. It is my humble job to make a short introductory opening to set the tone of the proceedings to come, which I beg to do with the kind permission of the revered Gurujans.

It is an acknowledged fact that the standards of excellence that the ancient Indian thinkers set for themselves and which they invariably achieved were the highest in every field of human endeavour, and so it was in the field of education and learning. Kalidasa has described the ideal teacher in his famous play ' MALAVIKAGNIMITRA' " Some people achieve great learning and achievement themselves, whereas others have the ability to transmit this learning and achievement into others. But the person in whom both these qualities converge together is the best of the teachers."

Though such was the high standing of our teachers, they neither expected nor encouraged a dumb acceptance of their teachings by their students. They fully realized that for the proper development of thought a spirit of enquiry and critical analysis was necessary without which nothing worthwhile can be achieved in the field of learning. It is therefore that we find in the 'PRASHNOPNISHAD' when Ashvatayan asks a very complex and complicated question to Pippalada his Guru. Pippalada instead of rebuking him for posing question as any of the spiritual Gurus of today would do, praises him. In the beginning Pippalada in great humility, tells the Rushikumars that they should stay in the ashram for one year and thereafter they could ask him whatever questions they wished and he, Pippalada would attempt to answer them. It was such men who took Indian thought to great heights in the past.

Today, the entire field of Indian Philosophy appears to have become sterile. Barring a few exceptions again of the past like Dr.Surendranath Dasgupta, Lokmanya Tilak, Dr.Radhakrishnan there is a little trace of genuine scholarship, a spirit of enquiry and ability of critical analysis. It is and shall be our humble endeavour to make all efforts possible through all channels, one of which is by arranging and organizing programs like the present one. And we strongly believe that these efforts on our part shall give a birth to a new renaissance in Indian thought.

Too difficult the task may seem to be, but we must repose our faith in the teacher and give them the freedom which they deserve.

Jai Hind.

Speech 3

Dear Comrades,

I have come here today to be amongst you to express my views on the presidential election and 'a would be candidate' for the post both the subject and a person uppermost in my mind at this moment. I expected a larger strength at this gathering. Nevertheless small is always attentive and committed, I take it that way.

A question was asked in one of the industry seminars as to what can be called a wonderful happening of 21st century in our country? In a matured democracy like India, an economist, without any political inkling has become the Prime Minister and again he is the one who precisely knows what Indian economy is and what needs to be done to scale it up further. Further a scientist of very high caliber not a leader of masses could chair for the full term the most coveted post of the President. By any yardstick, these are certainly good happenings on political front.

Why not carry these good precedents and a legacy is a question that is fast gaining ground at the moment on Indian political scene. And when it comes to choosing the next president, why not an engineer, a successful businessman, en ethical professional be persuaded for a next in line President. Narayan Murthy presently the Chairman and the Chief mentor of Infosys aptly fits the bill. Murthy the businessman has ably graced the responsibility of a Chairman of the board of IIM, Ahmedabad and has also served as a member of the board of Reserve Bank of India.

Our present President, most revered and respected Dr.Kalam may adore the post as long as it suits both the country in general and himself in particular. However if political obligations require making a choice of any other visionary, I suppose Murthy's candidature cannot be ignored. This would also continue the good trend of having non – political figure for the top posts.

As many of you know, Murty a man of unparallel vision dreamt of Infosys and chased his dream for an unmatched success. In a period of building success, the suggestion came from his colleagues to take Sudha Murthy on board as she too was well armed with requisite educational background. To that, Murthy firmly and politely said 'NO'. He advocated his no stand saying, 'A success in any field requires one's hundred per cent and that a couple in a board may not stand to that test'. This is yet another rare virtue to be held in high esteem and need to be weighed in a nose diving and hereditary ruled politics. I feel the ethics Murthy professed during his active Infosys days is sure to deter him from letting the politics sway from the chosen path. We need this pure sole in politics.

'The measure of life, after all is not its duration but its donation'. Murthy's Infosys foundation is working in the line with the said famous quote. Sudha Murthy stands as a steadfast towering woman behind that noble foundation. However the inspiration and the requisite resources are pumped in from Murty's Infosys. Murthy created wealth but with huge social responsibility and he runs it like Mahatma Gandhi's trusteeship. Gandhi said once, 'One needs to create wealth to wipe out the tears of poor'. Murthy and his Infosys team is instrumental in creating sustainable livelihood opportunities and I believe it is a right step in that direction. I say further that Murthy truly epitomizes that virtue.

'Murthy essentially symbolizes a change in the image of India showing it as the brain trust of the world'. Said Anand Mahindra.

The single virtue of Murthy that stands apart in political arena and lifts him above all is, he knows when to quit. He set an example of quitting the functional executive post at Infosys giving way to another able young person.

That noble attitude, that simplicity, and that proven performance in a chosen field makes Murthy a right candidate to run for president poll. And if this happens, the happening would send the appropriate signals to the whole world that Murthy heading the Government, we also mean business.

In US and outside US, everyone talks about Bush's business minded attitude when he declares a war against a particular country. Let us not under weigh this approach, not through war though. Is governing a country synonymous to running a business ? Only time will tell us.

I am grateful for giving me an opportunity to interact with such a highly perceptive and influential audience.

Jai Hind.

11. Some More Speech Examples!

I always try to structure my speeches around the Opening – Middle – Summary – Closing bit and it helps me to remember the flow and narration as well.

Speech 1

Reading As A Hobby For Life

"There is no friend as loyal as book." These are not my words but those of the famous author Ernest Hemingway. Louisa May Alcott, author of Little Women, takes it a step further and says, 'Good Books, like good friends, are few and chosen; the more selective, the more enjoyable!'

Good Evening,

Toastmaster of the day and all my fellow Toastmasters! A long time back, when I was staying in a hostel, my friends would hate me for not going out anywhere with them as I was a bookworm. They ask me even today 'Why are you always buried in books?' And here is what I tell them.

As proclaimed by the French philosopher, Rene Descartes, the reading of all good books is like having a conversation with the finest men of the past centuries.

I remember, in school, we read classics like 'Jane Eyre', 'Pride and Prejudice' and 'A Tale of Two Cities' and it had a profound impact on the way we studied English and History. Three years back, I was in Paris on a work assignment with colleagues. During the weekend, we visited historical monuments in Paris with a tour guide. This guide was a nice Frenchman, but could not handle the questions posed by co-tourists and colleagues. I stepped in confidently and helped him explain everyone the French Revolution, the Guillotine and the massacres. How was I able to do this? This was possible because I made books my best friend!

What this means to us is by reading books, we gain knowledge and can lead and take a superior edge in any debate. And this earned virtue helps us in our professional lives too.

Those who say "You Live Only Once" have never read a book. We all have only this life as we know it and we can live other lives in this life all by reading books. Let me give an example: In the summer of 1996, a grave tragedy occurred on Mount Everest. Sixteen mountaineers died the same day in an attempt to conquer the mountain. I knew this because I read the harrowing true story in a book called 'Into Thin Air' by Jon Krakauer and this book still makes me sad when I read it. It has also proved to be the catalyst for my trekking into the Himalayan region. With repeat reading of selective true stories and biographies, one can live the life of great souls. What this means to us is that we will be able to broaden our horizons and our perspectives and we can think big.

Reading a book builds imagination and helps us to visualize.

I used to read aloud to my son, when he was four years old. Gradually he developed the habit of reading books, but somewhere along the way, his play station gadget caught his fancy and that became the important thing in his life. Books naturally took a backseat. However I am confident that this crazy age phase will soon move off his mind. Recently, I came across a book 'Three Cups of Tea' by Greg Mortenson and I picked up an extra copy for my son. This book describes how a mountaineer trying to climb second tallest mountain – the Karakoram in Pakistan – lost his way while coming down. His return journey was troublesome. He was dehydrated and hungry and he stumbled into an impoverished Pakistan village where he stayed for more than ten days recuperating. That stay changed his life forever. He was moved by the plight and poverty of the villagers and their kindness. He decided to build a school for them. He returned back and he built not one but fifty five schools in the remote areas of Pakistan and Afghanistan for those who had no access to even primary education. The book tells us about the hardships he faced and the obstacles he overcame to achieve all that he thought. It is an inspiring book and I read it aloud this to my son. I am happy to say that my son Aditya has decided to buy this book as a birthday gift for his friends. Apart from this benefit, there is a divine purpose in buying the first copy of the book; a girl child receives a set of school books out of that money.

What this means to us is by reading aloud to our children, we indirectly help in raising responsible and thinking citizens of future.

Finally in the words of Dr. Seuss, "The more you read, the more things you will know. The more you learn, the more places you will go!"

In today's hectic pace of life, we may not have the time to do things that we wish. But let us introduce our children to one of the best friends with high potential; that is books.

Thank you!

Speech 2

My Dad – My Hero!

A wife will do a thousand things but she will never be the queen of her husband's heart. A daughter will make thousand mistakes and yet she will be her father's princess!

Good Evening to all such daughters and all such fathers! Yesterday was father's day and in its celebration – it is all about my father – my Baba!

Unstoppable! Unshakeable!! Unbreakable!!! The first picture that comes to the mind is a tall mountain. And that is what my dad is – taller than the tallest mountain!

But this is not a singular opinion of a daughter – rather this is what his ex-colleagues and relatives think about him, even today! He has carved a niche for himself – What exactly has made this unique identity?

Well, today he is a young man of eighty years only! I call him a young man, because for the last thirty five years, he has not lived a single day without swimming at least a kilometre every morning. Swimming has fortified him with stamina and strength.

He was born as the eldest son in a freedom fighter's family, brother to nine siblings. He studied up to inter-grade eleven and was a merit listed student. However money was so scarce and so was food… He had to give up studies to support his father in bringing up the family. This was a colossal sacrifice on his part apart from other small sacrifices. He found love and support in my mom and together they lived and are living a contented life but it was never a smooth ride. They have both struggled and worked very hard and ensured that their daughters received the best education, best books to read and a right atmosphere for adventure in life. Today they are proud parents of a Doctor and an Engineer.

The mountains have always consumed dad! Hiking and trekking have always lured him to explore the unknown! He has set his foot on many peaks along with his colleagues in the Sahyadri Mountains of Maharashtra. He has continuously won the 'Best Hiker' award in the last eight years of service in his company. He has also trekked in the Himalayan foothills of Himachal Pradesh and Uttaranchal, in India. I have accompanied him on few of these treks and they have been the most enchanting, enthralling and engrossing moments of my life!

In 1998, he undertook the rigorous Kailash – Mansarovar trek, conducted by the Indian Government. He was part of the sixth batch. The same year saw the twelfth batch of trekkers perish in a massive landslide. The famous dancer, ProtimaBedi and two of Dad's friends were among the people who died. This tragedy compelled Dad to write a guide book on Kailash – Mansarovar tour. It was a complete sell-out and currently running into its third edition.

My Dad officially retired at 58 years of age but only for namesake. The same firm retained his services for the next twelve years with all the perks! This reflects how invaluable he was to his company.

His zest for reading and learning has not slowed down with age. He still dreams of being a Mechanical Engineer in his next life. Imagine that! I was tired of studying in this life and he wants another life, just to study! On his last visit to Dubai, he pestered me to teach him on 'how to use a laptop'. The next thing I heard was – he went back home in Mumbai and bought himself a brand new laptop. His first book was completed using a Typewriter, the second edition using a desktop computer and the third edition using a laptop. He regularly emails me but is still figuring out how to send attachments.

People generally do not like hearing the truth, but Dad has never hesitated to say things the way they are. His honesty and straight forward nature has earned him respect and affection from all those who know him. His both son-in-law's grudgingly admire him and call him James Bond behind his back!

It is said that adversities and experiences make a person bitter or better! My Baba chose to be a better person!

Thank you.

Speech 3

Life Lessons

"Mistakes are guidelines and opportunities to learn how to do things better in life." Good morning everyone! My life is all about mathematics – I am constantly trying to add to my income, minus my weight, divide my time and avoid multiplying! But it has also taught me a lot of lessons and here are a few of them.

1st – Life is like an ocean, calm or rough, but always beautiful!

I remember I was in Grade Six and it was the History class. I saw my friend Rubina, pass a chit to someone in the class. She was caught and got a scolding from the teacher. I thought nothing more about it. The next day a Parent – Teacher meeting was scheduled. After the meeting my dad came home furious and was angry with me. He was told that I was misbehaving and passing chits in the class. I defended myself and told him, I did not do it. It was Rubina who played that mischief. My dad did not get convinced. He punished me by making me write "I shall not do anything wrong in the class" a hundred times in my notebook. Next day, I showed that script to my History Teacher. She realized her mistake and apologized to me and my dad. Dad had tears in his eyes and I had anger. I remember this incident very clearly as it taught me that 'truth is eternal'; it may be a bitter pill to swallow but it preserves. That day, I had taken a vow that I will always speak the truth, no matter what! As I grew up, I now understand that while I speak the truth– it may not always be the politically correct thing to say. As a result, I have collected very few close friends, over the years.

2nd – Life is like a mountain, hard to climb. But once you get on the top, the view is amazing!

I was on a trek with Dad in Garhwal, Uttaranchal in the year 1996. We had started early morning and trekked from Gangotri to Gaumukh and then to Tapovan. We headed back the same afternoon and reached an ashram in Bhojbasa, a tiny village on the way. Tired, dusty and hungry after walking almost twenty two kilometres, all we wanted was food and rest. Unfortunately the ashram had exhausted all its food supplies and all we could get was a cup of tea, made with Yak milk. Being the typical restless teenager, I screamed and made a big fuss for not having the food. I stepped out of the ashram hungry and angry, and saw the sky and the three peaks of Bhagirath mountains, illuminated by the golden-red rays of the setting sun! It was a spectacle and my joy knew no bounds. I had no camera but the image got embossed in my mind forever. There was no food and no place to stretch and yet the most beautiful sunset from the high peaks that I had witnessed gave me bellyful. It was an awesome experience that provided me an enriched lesson of life.

3rd – We have two ears to listen more and only one mouth to talk less! But we often end up doing exactly the opposite! Listening is a big challenge; it calls for your mindful attention. Let me illustrate with a simple incidence.

I was in the final year of my Engineering degree. We were attending campus interviews. One corporate firm had short listed fifteen of us. We were divided into two groups for group discussion. The topic for discussion was 'Globalization' and I knew absolutely nothing about the subject tabled for discussion. A couple of smart candidates from my group initiated the discussion like rapid fire and the rest of us were trying to act interested and make sense in the ongoing talk. Our acting stance did not last long. I gave up along with others. I felt safe to not listen further. The coordinator of the discussion suddenly asked the two of the rapid talkers to stop and looked at the list and said, 'Shilpa, what do you think of the discussion?' I was jolted out of my day dream and I was like – what do I think about what? It was an embarrassing moment for me. I was of course disqualified for further rounds. I learnt the value of listening.

Finally, after all the additions and subtractions of life, I feel, 'Errors and mistakes are opportunities and serve as guidelines to do things better'.

Thank You.

12. Tips On Power Dressing For Impact!

"A company without any advertisement is like a man winking at a woman in the dark!"

Power Dressing is the practice of dressing in a style intended to show that one holds an important position in business, politics, etc.

"Dress for the job you want" says an old proverb. Today's power dresser knows that clothes are an important part of projecting an image of success and confidence in the corporate world.And first impressions always matter.

For the Man:

- Business formal implies a business suit.
- In a single breasted business suit, buttons can be left open for comfort when you are not in front of the audience. But in front of the audience, the style is to button up only the first one.
- A double breasted suit requires all the buttons to be done up.
- Lapels, if any, should always be kept outside.
- It is always contrast colours that work best with the shirt and suit combination.
- Wear only one set of stripes in the suit – shirt – tie combination.
- o If the shirt has stripes, wear plain suit and plain or patterned tie.
- o If suit has stripes, wear plain shirt and plain or patterned tie.
- o If you wear a striped tie, then wear a plain shirt and a plain suit.

- When wearing a tie, the tie length is important. The correct length to wear is thetip of the tie extends up to the middle of the belt buckle. Anything longer or shorter looks out of place. It is illustrated in the picture below.

PROPER TIE LENFTH GUIDE

- White socks look best at school and during sports activities. Coloured socks are the norm at all other times.
- Only half inch of the shirt sleeve should show below the jacket. It is as illustrated in the picture below.

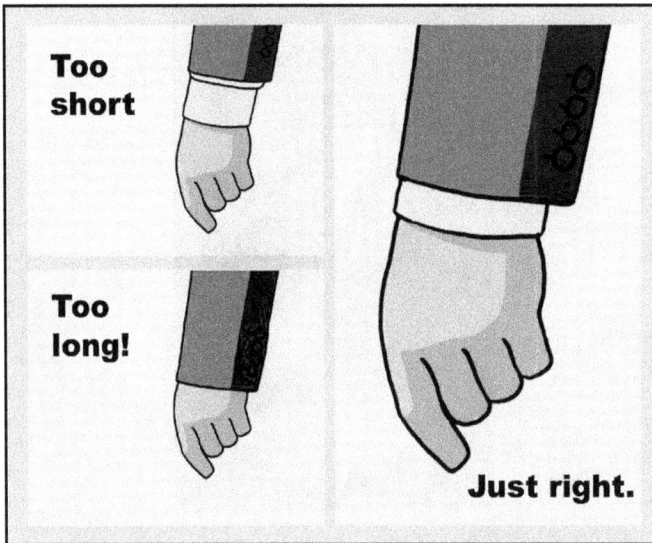

Too short

Too long!

Just right.

What do Princess Diana, Naomi Campbell and Margaret Thatcher have in common? They were all masters of power dressing! Power dressing, as a new fashion phenomenon, has its symbols in public figures such as Hillary Clinton, Michelle Obama, Christine Lagarde and many more.

Christine Lagarde, MD of the International Monetary Fund

Michelle Obama, First Lady of the White House

Margaret Thatcher above all was one of the first to incorporate the spirit of power suits. Her personal style was, according to Vogue, reinvented in order to make her appearance appropriate for the role of Prime Minister. She was Britain's first female icon to pioneer at the same time politics and fashion, setting an example for women who would have come next. She claimed her style to be "never flashy, just appropriate".

Former Prime Minister of United Kingdom, Margaret Thatcher

Dress sensibly, comfortably and sharp to project the confidence that you feel from within and the world will be yours!

13. A Wake Up Call!

"The happiness lies in sufferings, troubles and sorrow. The sad state of mind puts one to go through the self-analysing process; It makes one introspective; Its' sustaining frees the disorders occurred in mind and body; It cleanses the inner instincts. The thoughts of sorrow help recollect the purpose of life and realize one's own divine inner form. Happiness dawns when sufferings surfeits adequately like the sprout comes after struggle and breaking of the seed. In summary, without intolerable grief, comfort and joy would never pave way. We need to understand that sad days are sure to turn on; for a happy track. It is a science fact that if there exists a shadow; there has to be a light ahead of it. And hence one should be ready to get admitted to a GOD designated school of sorrow as and when it warrants"- From the teachings of Sant Kalavati Devi.

Sometimes we wonder why GOD does not grant us a life of ease, free of burdens. Life is filled with many problems. Why do we struggle with health problems, financial, relationship and emotional problems?

Here is an example from nature. The eagle finds the tallest tree or highest mountain ledge to build its nest. The eagle lays the first layer of the nest with sharp objects such as thorns and stones. Next, the eagle covers the layer of sharp objects with soft material, such as wood, feathers and animal fur. As the baby bird hatch, the soft layer of the nest surround them. After they grow a bit, the mother eagle takes the nest material and mixes it up. The jumbled mass becomes a mixture of sharp objects and soft ones. Some of the sharp edges even cut the baby birds' skin. Soon, the mother stops putting food from her mouth into the babys' mouths. Their comfortable world becomes painful. They are hungry and in pain from the sharp edges cutting into their bodies. The discomfort becomes so acute that the babies begin to fly away to get out of the nest. This beautiful analogy from nature explains the value of suffering in our lives.

Most people turn to GOD only in times of trouble. When they are faced with intolerable pain, an incurable illness, a devastating loss, or a financial disaster, they find that life is not great as they thought it was. It is during those times of pain and crises that we begin to question if there is GOD, and ask, what is the purpose of this life?

Suffering has the value of turning our attention to the lord. Without it most people would not give GOD a second thought. They would live and die without even thinking about GOD. Suffering makes us pray GOD. When we suddenly loose all that we own, our stocks drop, or we loose our home, we begin to seek GOD. Misfortunes make us turn to a higher power for help.

Sometimes when we become too complacent, GOD may shake things up a bit to make us do our spiritual work. GOD wants all of the baby eagles to soar. GOD wants us to soar from this physical region to the astral, from the astral to the causal region, from the causal to the supra-causal region, and from their to return to the highest spiritual realms.

GOD may do whatever it takes to help all the eagles fly and return home through meditation. It is a wake-up call to teach us that we should not be too comfortable in the physical world.

We can wake up to the sharpness of life so that we can rise from this physical world and soar into spiritual realms within. At times, GOD removes the soft coverings so we can be reminded that this life is painful and full of suffering.

The above stated realization will drive us to put in greater effort to meditate more and to soar to our home of true peace - From the teachings of Sant Rajinder Singh

*****

There was a queen named Madalsa. She inculcated the right 'Samskars' on her seven children and made them sage- the learned and ascetics. Eventually they all marched on their predetermined track. However for the youngest sibling, the queen had different plan. She wanted to create a prince for the throne. She made him acquainted to the various rituals of the kingdom. He was systematically made well-versed to the various branches of knowledge. Making him well equipped King and the Queen decided to walk off kingdom on salvation path. Moved by their decision the prince expressed his apprehension and concern of his future without their support. Queen tied a charm-an amulet on his wrist and advised him to read its contents when in need. In the course of time, he felt a need. He opened the amulet and read. It was inscribed 'These days will also take a turn around'. The prince got the message right! He successfully passed through the turbulent times he faced. Morale - The state of disservice and disorder give birth to its remedy too.

A mighty tree produces a beautiful ripe fruit. But as seasons passed by it let fall off its leaves. Out of that again springs the new branches and leaves. It is sprouting, its first leaves are already out, and a largely spread tree, the "Urdhvamulam" is here. This tough period through which we pass is all the more necessary.

The anxiety cropping out of sufferings becomes instrumental in nose-diving of our 'PURUSHARTHA' It makes one dull and non-active. During the state of sufferings, even the abstemious 'KARMAS' take the course of ebb-tide. And hence, let wilful sustenance, peace and wisdom prevails in suffering; goes the saying.

A Mahabharata empress Kunti consciously pleaded for sufferings and grief, stating that this would perpetually keep her in the worship of Lord Krishna. This asking is unusual, extra-ordinary, remarkable and phenomenal. There is no parallel to this asking in the history of bonding between a worshipper and The Almighty.

Sant Kabir says, 'Sukh me bhaje to dukkh kayeko hove' When we are rich and living in the lap of luxury, we do not think about GOD. If people were too happy and comfortable in their physical existence, they would never seek GOD. Morale is worshipping GOD is not a one time penance. 'Nirantar Nam-

Smaran' Kabir says, is a must and incessant in all states of pleasant (sukh) and unpleasant (dukkh) experiences.

God, though everywhere, we get to know him more during troubled times.

Troubles are the wake up calls from GOD!

!! END !!

" Reading maketh a full man, conference { speaking } a ready man and writing an exact man" - Francis Bacon

About the Authors

Mukund Puranik is a Commerce & Law Graduate with Post Qualification in Management Studies. Post his retirement, he has developed a flair for writing and contributed number of columns in print media and gave talks in various forums. He had organised series of events where prominent speakers were invited to give speeches on socio-political subjects under the banner 'Sushrut - Pune'.

Mukund Puranik

Shilpa Nazar is a trained Computer Engineer with a Masters' in Computing Systems.She has more than 18 years of experience being a University Faculty as a teacher, trainer,coach and mentor. As a Faculty, her focus has always been to help her students to reach their goals and achieve success. As a Trainer, she has helped participants with their understanding, which has helped them to perform efficiently and productively at work. Her passion for public speaking led her to leadership and skills development. Working as an independent Coach in Dubai, since 2006, her role is to get people to identify their own strengths as communicators. She has helped more than 900 participants to realize their potential and become positively motivated. She is an avid trekker and has explored and hiked through the Himalayan terrain in India. Her desire to excel and adapt in her role have facilitated her to help build participant's self-confidence.

Shilpa Nazar

* 9 7 8 9 3 8 6 4 0 1 0 4 5 *